W9-AZX-685

The Kneaded Loaf

◆

A Guide to Contemporary Bread Making

◆

RED STAR ✪

New York London Toronto Sydney Tokyo Singapore

The Kneaded Loaf
RED STAR® Yeast & Products
A Division of Universal Foods Corporation

Publication Manager: Brian C. Thornquist

Food Editor: Glenna W. Vance

Associate Food Editors: Alice J. Pearson, Joyce M. Graf,
Patricia P. Waldoch

Test Kitchen Coordinator: Alice J. Pearson

Contributing Editor: Thomas N. Lacalamita

Food Stylists: Glenna W. Vance, Alice J. Pearson

Photography: Photographic Images, William Lemke

Cover & Book Design: Sundberg & Associates Inc

Project Coordinators: Media Tech Enterprises, Inc.

An *Original* Publication of POCKET BOOKS

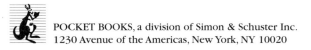

POCKET BOOKS, a division of Simon & Schuster Inc.
1230 Avenue of the Americas, New York, NY 10020

Copyright © 1995 RED STAR® Yeast & Products

All rights reserved, including the right to reproduce this book
or portions thereof in any form whatsoever. For information,
address Pocket Books, 1230 Avenue of the Americas, New York,
NY 10020.

ISBN: 0-671-56845-0

First Pocket Books trade paperback printing November 1995

10 9 8 7 6 5 4 3 2 1

POCKET and colophon are registered trademarks of
Simon & Schuster Inc.
Red Star is a registered trademark of Universal Foods
Corporation.

Printed in the U.S.A.

Table of Contents

Chapter 5 / Rolls, Flat Breads, and Braided Loaves

Chapter 6 / Loaves for Celebration

Foreword

Bread, both nourishing and satisfying, is one of the few foods that knows no cultural boundaries. At one time, soft white bread was taken for granted by many as the definition of this staple food. Over the past ten years, Americans have been rediscovering yeast bread and its many flavors, textures, and shapes. Coarse, whole-grain peasant loaves and buttery-rich sweet breads are now being made by many home bakers, who up to a few years ago would never have considered making homemade bread. Now the technique for making homemade bread has evolved from the traditional method of hand kneading the dough to using small electrical appliances like bread machines, electric mixers, and food processors. Ingredients like bread flour and dry yeast are readily available in almost every supermarket, which makes it easier than ever to bake bread at home.

Americans have been rediscovering yeast bread and its many flavors, textures, and shapes.

The Kneaded Loaf is a collection of recipes from RED STAR® Yeast & Products. As the only American-owned, American-made manufacturer of yeast in the United States, RED STAR has been serving the home bread baker for well over 110 years. This cookbook represents the type of breads Americans are enjoying today. The recipes range from simple, yet basic, Old-Fashioned Buttermilk White and Hearty Rye Bread to hand-shaped sweet breads. Easy-to-follow instructions are provided for use with the popular bread machine and the more traditional mixer method, which includes hand-held mixers, stand mixers, and food processors.

To ensure that your breads and baked goods come out perfect every time, the introduction provides baking techniques, tips, and suggestions developed and acquired over the years. In addition, there is a quick checklist, Improving Your Breads, at the end of the recipe section.

Introduction

Years ago, the first thing people did when they went on a diet was to cut back on bread, cereals, and pastas. Little did we know that the complex carbohydrates they provide are a vital source of dietary fiber, minerals, and vitamins necessary for lowering the incidence of chronic illnesses, such as cancer, heart disease, and diabetes. In fact, according to the National Academy of Sciences, the National Institute of Health, and the American Heart Association, complex carbohydrates should constitute 55 percent of our total daily caloric intake. The United States Department of Agriculture recommends six to eleven servings a day (a slice of bread equals a single serving). Bread, therefore, in all of its natural goodness, can and should be a vital part of a healthy diet.

The Kneaded Loaf provides the home bread baker with a wide variety of delicious breads to be served any time of the day. For the most part, the breads are low in fat and cholesterol and high in much-needed soluble and insoluble fiber, essential components of a well-balanced, healthy diet. On special occasions, or when you have the desire to splurge, you can celebrate with some richer sweet breads.

Chapter 1
The Knead to Know

Bread Making Methods

IF YOU HAVE EVER MADE BREAD BY HAND, you are in for a real surprise. Most likely you have bread-making machines in your kitchen without even knowing it: hand-held mixers, stand mixers, and even food processors make bread baking fun. All you have to do is measure the ingredients and follow the easy instructions in the book. Before you know it, you will be enjoying one of the greatest possible pleasures from your kitchen—a loaf of wonderful, homemade bread. Of course, bread machines make the process even easier.

BREAD MACHINES first made their appearance in American kitchens in the late 1980s. This Japanese invention, more than any other, has revolutionized how Americans perceive making homemade bread today. The user measures the ingredients and puts them in the bread pan. After he or she chooses the cycle desired and presses START, the bread machine does the rest. It mixes and kneads the dough, lets it rise, and then bakes the bread automatically. The bread machine can also be used to make yeast dough that the home baker can then hand shape and bake in a conventional oven.

HAND-HELD MIXERS can be found in almost every household. An invaluable tool for whipping potatoes and making cake batters, they are often overlooked for making yeast dough. A hand-held mixer can be used to blend the liquids with some of the dry ingredients and prepare a thick batterlike dough. The remaining flour is stirred in by hand to make a firm dough before kneading. Using a hand-held mixer in the beginning reduces the length of kneading time.

STAND MIXERS come in bowl sizes ranging from 3 to 5 quarts and are similar to those used by commercial bakers to make yeast dough. The powerful mixing action, first with beaters then with dough hook(s), allows the dough to be made entirely by machine.

FOOD PROCESSORS another popular kitchen appliance, are typically used for chopping and shredding. Due to their speed and the design of the blade, food processors can be used to quickly make excellent yeast dough.

Ingredients

SINCE THE CHEMISTRY OF BREAD MAKING is the transformation of ingredients into bread, it is a good idea to understand how the ingredients work together.

Yeast

YEAST, THE LEAVENING AGENT USED to make bread dough rise, is a single-cell organism that grows and multiplies as it ferments sugar. The fermentation process produces ethyl alcohol and carbon dioxide. The gases are trapped in the dough in the form of small bubbles which force the dough to rise.

There are two basic types, or strains, of RED STAR® Yeast available to the home bread baker: RED STAR® Active Dry Yeast and QUICK·RISE™ Active Dry Yeast (also known as RED STAR® Instant Active Dry Yeast). Active Dry Yeast is the original all-natural yeast that has been used by generations of bread bakers. Although the same yeast is available in some supermarkets in the cake form of fresh compressed yeast, dry yeast is now preferred by grocers and bakers because of its longer shelf life. QUICK·RISE™ Active Dry Yeast can also be used. When used with any of the mixer methods, it shortens the time of the first and second risings; the dough can rise up to 50 percent faster. When QUICK·RISE™ Active Dry Yeast is used in most bread machines, the amount of yeast called for in the recipe is reduced. Otherwise, the dough will rise faster than the bread machine cycles progress. A rule of thumb is to use ½ teaspoon of QUICK·RISE™ Active Dry Yeast per cup of flour.

When bread is mixed by hand, the yeast is dissolved in a warm liquid (110° to 115° F) before being added to the dry ingredients. Due to the efficient mixing and kneading action of today's kitchen appliances, this step is unnecessary and is therefore eliminated. It is essential, however, that the liquids be at the appropriate temperature for the bread-making method used (see Liquids, page 12).

Unopened packages of yeast have a one-year shelf life from the date they are packaged. The "best if used by" date is printed on the outside of the package. Since yeast is very perishable when exposed to air, moisture, and/or warmth, all opened packages of yeast must be refrigerated or frozen in an airtight container. Under refrigeration, the life of yeast is about six weeks and when frozen, six months.

Should you suspect that your yeast has declined in rising power, it can be tested as follows. In a 1-cup measuring cup, dissolve 1 teaspoon of granulated sugar in ½ cup warm water (110° to 115° F). Sprinkle 1 packet (2¼ teaspoons) of yeast over the surface. Stir and let sit ten minutes. In three to four minutes, the yeast will have absorbed enough liquid to activate and will begin to rise to the surface. If, at the end of ten minutes, the yeast has multiplied to the top of the container and has a rounded crown, it is very active and may be used immediately. *Remember to deduct ½ cup of liquid from the recipe to adjust for the water used in the test.*

Flour and Grains

Bread Flour

BREAD IS TRADITIONALLY MADE with wheat flour because wheat is the only grain that contains a sufficient amount of the type of protein that forms gluten which holds the dough together and gives it the needed elasticity to rise and grow. There are two basic types of wheat grown in North America, hard and soft. Hard wheat has a higher level of protein, making it the wheat of choice for most yeast doughs. Soft wheat has a low protein content and is best suited for making pastries and cakes.

All-purpose flour, a blend of hard and soft wheat, is the most commonly purchased and used flour. It provides satisfactory results when mixing and kneading dough by hand. However, for the bread-making methods given in this cookbook, use high-protein bread flour unless the recipe calls for all-purpose flour. Bread flour is available in most supermarkets in 5-pound and 10-pound bags.

As the flour is mixed with the other ingredients in the recipe, the protein comes in contact with the liquids to become gluten, and an interlocking network of elastic strands are formed, which trap the gases produced by the yeast. As the dough is kneaded, the gluten network increases and strengthens, allowing the dough to support the weight and shape of the loaf.

Since bread machines, stand mixers, and food processors knead more vigorously than human hands, it is possible to overknead the dough and ultimately break down the gluten. The bread will be small and dense. Therefore, it is important to knead the dough only as long as the recipe states. Never continue kneading the dough to the point that it begins to break down, losing its ball-like shape or tearing into ragged edges when stretched. Well-kneaded dough should stay together in a soft, smooth ball. Dough is ready for rising once it has an elastic consistency.

Whole Wheat Flour

WHOLE WHEAT FLOUR IS GROUND from the entire wheat kernel, which contains all of the natural nutrients. Breads baked from whole wheat flour have a distinctive nutty flavor derived from the bran and germ of the wheat. Because whole wheat flour is not as refined as bread flour, breads made with 100 percent whole wheat, or a large percentage of it, may not rise as high as those made solely with bread flour. To compensate for this in the whole wheat recipes, other ingredients like eggs and cottage cheese have been included. They can help to make the dough lighter, rise higher, and have better texture and taste.

Usually the whole wheat flour sold in most supermarkets is milled from a variety of hard and soft red wheats. It may be used in combination with bread flour to make a lighter loaf. Whole wheat flours may also be milled from hard white wheat varieties. They have a mild, mellow flavor and are excellent when making a 100 percent whole wheat bread recipe. Hard white wheat flours are available in some supermarkets and mail-order catalogs or through specialty and health food stores.

Other Grains

RYE HAS BEEN VALUED for hundreds of years by northern and eastern Europeans for making bread. However, it has a very low protein content and is always mixed with a substantially larger amount of bread flour in order for the bread to rise.

Breads and other baked goods made with buckwheat are very popular in parts of the United States. Buckwheat flour, which is ground from the seeds of the buckwheat plant, is not a variety of wheat flour nor does it contain any gluten. Nevertheless, small quantities may be substituted for bread flour to make a delicious, homey loaf. The same holds true for flours from other grains like corn, oats, rice, barley, and soy.

Due to the oils in grain, flours stored at room temperature may turn rancid over time and impart an off taste to the bread. To store flours properly over an extended period of time, place them in plastic freezer bags or air tight plastic containers and freeze. Avoid storing flour in self-defrosting refrigerators, since they tend to dry out flour. Flour must be at room temperature before using.

Liquids

LIQUID INGREDIENTS PLAY three important roles in bread making. They rehydrate and dissolve the yeast granules. They help to blend and bind the ingredients together. And they allow the gluten to develop so that the dough will be elastic. In addition to water, liquids include milk, buttermilk, sour cream, eggs, cottage cheese, fruit juices, and fruit and vegetable purees. Fats and liquid sweeteners also add moisture.

Accurate liquid temperature is of utmost importance as it directly influences the yeast activity. The appropriate temperature depends on the bread-making method being used. For example, since the kneading action of a bread machine takes place in a closed container, the considerable friction and consequent heat generated make a very warm environment for the dough. Therefore, the liquid ingredients should be no warmer than approximately 80° F—slightly warmer than room temperature yet cooler than body temperature. With the mixer methods, the liquids have to be considerably warmer (120° to 130° F).

Liquid ingredients can be mixed together and brought to the appropriate temperature in a small saucepan over low heat or in a mixing bowl in a microwave oven. Always check the temperature of the liquids with a thermometer before adding them to the dry ingredients. If the liquids are too hot, there is a risk of killing the yeast or overstimulating it to multiply too quickly, thus causing the dough to overproof (rise inconsistently). On the other hand, if the liquids are too cool, the yeast will not activate properly and the dough will not rise sufficiently. A thermometer is a must for consistently good quality breads.

Do not heat the eggs with the other liquids, since they may begin to cook. The eggs, however, need to be at room temperature. Take them out of the refrigerator one to two hours before baking or place the uncracked eggs in a small bowl of warm water for a few minutes. The standard measurement for an egg is ¼ cup. A large egg will equal this amount. If the egg is less than ¼ cup, add water to the ¼ cup measurement. If the egg is more than ¼ cup, adjust another liquid amount to compensate. To save leftover egg white or egg yolk, mix with 1 tablespoon of water and put in an ice cube tray. Freeze and then store in plastic bags. It will come in handy when a recipe calls for an egg yolk or egg white wash. Simply thaw one cube in a small dish.

Milk and buttermilk give bread a softer crumb and crust, which is desired in some types of breads. When making bread or yeast dough in a bread machine, do not use the delay timer if the recipe contains eggs or dairy products such as milk or cheese. They can spoil.

Juices and purees add sugar, flavor, and color to bread.

Fats

MOST BREADS CONTAIN a small quantity of fat. If a fat is liquid at room temperature, it is called oil; if solid at room temperature, shortening. Fat gives the dough richness and moisture, but more importantly, it makes the bread tender. Fat coats the flour particles so the elastic formation slows down; it makes the gluten strands slippery so the gas bubbles can move easily; and it gives the final product a finer grain.

Sugar and Salt

BESIDES ENHANCING AND ADDING FLAVOR to bread, sugar and salt are two key ingredients in dough development. Sugar comes in many forms like white and brown sugar, honey, molasses, and corn syrup; they may be interchanged successfully. Most artificial sweeteners cannot be fermented so they cannot be substituted for sugar. Remember, yeast needs sugar to grow and multiply. However, at high sugar levels the activity of yeast decreases. Sweet breads naturally include more sugar so as to enhance the flavor of the bread, but yield a dense, fine texture.

Certain doughs, like pizza, contain no added sugar. This is what gives pizza crust its characteristic chewy texture. Since the yeast can ferment only the limited amount of natural sugars found in the flour, the rising process is dramatically slowed.

While sugar helps the dough to rise, salt has the opposite effect. It inhibits the yeast activity and, therefore, assures that the dough rises evenly. Salt also strengthens the dough structure; eliminating the salt can result in a collapsed bread.

BREADS AND YEAST DOUGHS CAN BE FLAVORED with an endless variety of dried fruits, nuts, herbs, spices, and flavorings. For the most part, they will enhance the flavor and texture of the bread.

If ingredients such as raisins and nuts are added at the beginning of the dough-making process with the other dry ingredients, they may become chopped up during kneading. To prevent this from happening, add them toward the end of the kneading stage as indicated:

BREAD MACHINE METHOD: If your bread machine has a special program or setting for adding dried fruits and nuts, add them at the appropriate moment, in accordance with the manufacturer's instructions. This is usually near the end of the second kneading time.

HAND-HELD MIXER METHOD: Dried fruits and nuts should be added into the dough with the remaining flour; then the dough should be kneaded until smooth and elastic.

STAND MIXER METHOD: Dried fruits and nuts should be added into the dough with the remaining flour; then the dough should be kneaded until smooth and elastic.

FOOD PROCESSOR METHOD: Dried fruits and nuts should be added only after the dough has been kneaded; otherwise, the metal blade will cut them into tiny pieces.

Place them in the processor bowl and incorporate by pressing the pulse switch two or three times, just until mixed.

Bear in mind that certain ingredients may have a negative effect on dough. Two common culprits are cinnamon and garlic. Cinnamon is a natural preservative, so too much cinnamon in a recipe will counteract the properties of the yeast. Since cinnamon has such a rich flavor, there really is no need to use more than ½ teaspoon per cup of flour.

Garlic, which is often used in marinades to tenderize tough cuts of meat, has the same effect on gluten; it breaks down the elastic strands. Use sparingly.

Baking Techniques

Proper Measuring

BESIDES USING THE PROPER INGREDIENTS, it is also essential that they be measured correctly. Dry measuring cups and spoons do not have a lip so accurate measuring is achieved by the use of a flat edge knife to scrape off the excess. For measuring small quantities of sugar, salt, yeast, herbs, etc., scoop or sprinkle the ingredient into the appropriate measuring cup or spoon; level with the flat edge of a knife.

Flour is sifted many times before being packaged. During shipping, it settles and becomes compact. It is important not to dip the measuring cup into the flour bag; instead, scoop the flour lightly into a dry measuring cup. Using the flat edge of a knife, scrape off the excess to make the flour even with the rim of the measuring cup. This method will assure an accurate measurement. The amount of moisture in flour varies depending on the growing conditions of the grain, the milling process, and the storage. Therefore, it may be necessary to use more flour than called for in the recipe during the kneading time.

Liquid measurement containers come in several sizes and have a lip above the measuring line to prevent spills. They are translucent or transparent for easy reading. To use, place the cup on a level surface with the measurement line at eye level for accurate reading.

There are two ways to accurately measure shortening. The first uses cold water and mathematical skills. For example, to measure ⅓ cup of shortening, fill a 1-cup liquid measuring cup to the ⅔-cup mark with cold water. Carefully spoon pieces of shortening into the water until the water reaches the 1-cup mark. Pour off the water; there will be exactly ⅓ cup of shortening in the cup.

The second method requires the solid shortening to be packed into a dry measuring cup with a rubber spatula. Run the spatula through the shortening several times while packing to eliminate any air pockets. When the cup is full, level the contents using the flat edge of a knife.

Honey and molasses will easily slide off a measuring spoon if oil is first measured with the same spoon.

For best results, all dry ingredients should be at room temperature. The liquid ingredients should be at the appropriate temperature for the bread-making method that you are using (see Liquids, page 12). Sourdough starters should also be at room temperature.

Bread Machine Method

ALTHOUGH THE BREAD MACHINE WILL MIX, knead, and bake bread, it is absolutely necessary that you learn to recognize the condition of your dough. The ratio of flour to liquid is the most critical factor in any bread recipe, yet the most easily remedied. It is all right to open the machine to check the dough's consistency. Do this after about five minutes into the KNEAD cycle. The dough should be in a soft, tacky ball. If it is too dry, add liquid ½ to 1 tablespoon at a time; if it is too wet, add 1 tablespoon of flour at a time.

The Hand-Held Mixer Method and Kneading Dough by Hand

THE HAND-HELD MIXER METHOD PROVIDES a jump start to the development of the dough. It easily combines part of the flour, all of the other dry ingredients, and all of the liquids to form a batter. The liquid temperature is quite warm because the flour acts as a buffer to protect the yeast from the heat. Thus, the batter provides an excellent warm moist environment for the yeast to activate quickly, while part of the flour begins to form gluten strands. Combining the ingredients with the hand-held mixer lessens both the kneading time and the rising time. Additional flour is gradually added by hand to make a firm dough; the dough is then ready to knead.

To knead, place the dough on a lightly floured surface, turning it over several times to make it easier to handle. With curved fingers, fold the dough in half toward you. With the heel of your hand, push the dough down and away, firmly but lightly, in a rolling motion. Give the dough a quarter turn. Repeat folding, pushing, and turning until the dough is smooth on the outside and springy when pressed with the fingers.

Stand Mixer Method

THE STAND MIXER METHOD WILL MIX and knead the dough. However, it is important to know when the dough has been adequately kneaded. At the beginning of the kneading time, take off a walnut-sized ball of dough. Using both hands, hold the dough between the thumbs and forefingers and stretch it—much like stretching a balloon before blowing it up. At this time, the dough will probably tear easily. Toss the dough piece back into the mixer and repeat this process every couple of minutes. When the dough has been kneaded enough, it will not tear easily, but rather will stretch, and a translucent membrane will be visible when the dough is held up toward a light. This is known as a "gluten window." At this point, stop the mixer, remove the dough, and prepare it for rising.

A FOOD PROCESSOR PROVIDES an easy and lightening fast method of dough making. Simply place all dry ingredients in a processor bowl fitted with a steel blade. Secure the lid, start the machine, and pour the warmed liquids through the feeder tube while the motor is running. Watch closely, as dough will form a ball in about sixty seconds. Count! The dough ball will ride the blade and clean the sides of the bowl as it goes around. Turn off the machine promptly when this happens, open the lid, and check the dough. It should feel warm, soft, satiny-smooth, and elastic.

Rising and the Ripe Test

WHEN MAKING YEAST BREAD, the kneaded dough has to rise in order to let the yeast act and the dough develop. This step also improves the flavor and texture of the bread.

To rise, place the kneaded dough in a lightly oiled, large mixing bowl. The dough should be turned over to oil the top so that it does not dry out. Cover the bowl loosely with plastic wrap or foil and let the dough rise in a warm, draft-free location. The oven is an ideal place for this. For an electric oven or a gas oven with electronic ignition, heat the oven at the lowest setting for one minute, then turn off. In other gas ovens, the pilot light will provide enough warmth. The oven temperature should not exceed 90° F. during the rising time. Place a pan of very warm water toward the back of the oven to provide moisture. Place the bowl or pan of dough on the center rack and close the door.

Many factors, including the recipe, room temperature, and humidity, will determine how long it takes for the dough to rise. The best way to decide whether it has risen sufficiently and is ready to be punched down and shaped is to perform a "ripe test." Gently stick two fingers in the risen dough up to the second knuckle and take them out (photo, page 33). If the indentations remain, the dough is "ripe" and ready for punch down (photo, page 33). If not, cover and let rise longer.

Since the bread machine is a self-contained mixer, dough proofer, and oven, the appliance automatically takes care of all of these steps and the following procedures when making loaves of bread. However, if you plan to use the bread machine to make dough that will then be hand shaped, you will also need to read the following section.

Punching Down, Shaping, and Rising

AFTER THE DOUGH HAS RISEN in the mixing bowl, it has to be punched down to remove the gas bubbles before it can be shaped. Once the dough is approximately half its original size, knead it a couple of times and then let it rest, covered, for approximately five minutes. The gluten will relax and it will be easier to handle the dough for shaping.

After shaping the bread, cover it and let it rise again. This time the "ripe test" is simply a light fingertip touch to the side of the risen bread. If the indentation remains, the bread is ripe and ready for the oven (photo, page 33).

Baking and Cooling

YEAST DOUGH SHOULD ALWAYS BE BAKED on the center rack of a preheated, hot oven for the length of time specified in the recipe. During the first few minutes in the oven, the final expansion of the dough takes place. This is called "oven spring." The time-tested method of determining if the bread has baked sufficiently is to tap the crust lightly and listen for a hollow sound. A more accurate method is to insert an instant-read thermometer (available in most housewares departments) into the center of the bread. When the thermometer registers 190° F, remove the bread from the oven. If the crust is browning too quickly, cover the top with a tented sheet of foil.

After baking, remove the bread from the pan and place on a wire rack to cool. Cooling allows the structure of the bread to firm up. Slicing the bread while it is still hot will break down the structure. Use a serrated knife with a gentle sawing motion for cutting. An electric knife also works well.

Storing Dough and Bread

STORING BAKED BREADS IN THE REFRIGERATOR DRIES them out. To retain the freshness of crusty loaves of bread, store them unwrapped at room temperature. Once sliced, place in a paper bag. Soft-crusted loaves can be placed in a plastic bag. Homemade bread contains no preservatives; it usually stays fresh for a short period of time. When bread has lost its freshness, remember, there are croutons, bread crumbs, bread pudding—or your dog; dogs love hard bread.

Yeast dough can be chilled in the refrigerator or frozen in the freezer for later use.

Refrigeration

ALL DOUGHS CAN BE REFRIGERATED. Chilling dough slows the activity of the yeast, but it does not stop it completely. For this reason, it is necessary to punch the dough down one or two hours after it has been placed in the refrigerator. Once the dough has completely cooled, it needs to be punched down only once every twenty-four hours. Dough will last approximately three days in the refrigerator; however, it is best to use it within forty-eight hours.

After the dough is kneaded, place it in a tightly covered, large mixing bowl or self-sealing plastic bag before refrigerating. The refrigeration time is considered the first rise time. To use, remove the dough from the refrigerator, punch it down, and allow it to rest before shaping. The final rising will be longer than indicated in the recipe because the dough will still be cool. Bake according to the recipe directions.

Dough may also be refrigerated after it has been formed into the desired shape. Cover shaped loaves or rolls tightly and refrigerate up to twenty-four hours. Remove from the refrigerator, partially unwrap, and let rise until they pass the "ripe test" (see Punching Down, Shaping and Rising, page 17). Bake according to the recipe directions.

Freezing

YEAST DOUGH CAN ALSO BE FROZEN for later shaping and baking. After the dough has been kneaded, divide it into the sections needed for the finished product, for example, one loaf of bread, one pizza, one pan of rolls. Flatten each section into a 1-inch-thick disk. Place in self-sealing plastic bags and freeze. Dough can be kept in the freezer up to four weeks. For an even thaw, place it in the refrigerator overnight. Partially unwrap and place it on the counter for fifteen to twenty minutes to bring it to room temperature. Punch down the dough. Proceed with shaping and the second rising. Dough may also be moved directly from the freezer to the counter for a shorter thawing time. However, the edges will thaw faster than the center, so the dough will have to be worked some as it thaws.

Dough can also be frozen after being formed into the desired shape, before the second rising. Place shaped dough on a cookie sheet and place it in the freezer one hour to harden. Remove from freezer and wrap in plastic wrap or foil. Place in a self-sealing plastic bag and return it to the freezer. Dough can be kept frozen up to four weeks. To thaw, unwrap the dough and place it on a lightly greased cookie sheet. Lightly oil the top of the shaped dough and cover tightly with a piece of plastic wrap or foil. Thaw overnight in the refrigerator. Remove from refrigerator, partially unwrap, and bring to room temperature. Let the dough rise until it passes the "ripe test" (see Punching Down, Shaping, and Rising, page 17). Bake according to the recipe directions.

Baked, completely cooled breads can also be successfully frozen. Wrap first in plastic wrap or foil, then place in a self-sealing plastic bag. Freeze for six to eight weeks. Let thaw at room temperature, partially unwrapped to allow moisture to escape. Slicing bread before freezing will make it possible to take out a partial loaf at a time and will shorten the thawing time, as the slices can easily be separated. However, it may not stay as fresh for an extended period of freezing.

Chapter 2
Loaves For Everyday Dining

Homemade bread everyday? Yes! It is not only possible, but highly probable with the easy-to-make recipes found in this chapter. Start thinking about which bread to make and your imagination will be like a chain reaction sparking a renewed interest in meal planning. Bread making stimulates creativity for an exciting menu. Everyday stews, soups, and pastas will be more attractive to your palate if you begin to plan the bread course first.

Viennese Bread could accompany any spaghetti or lasagna entree, while Santa Fe Chili Bread would, as the name implies, enhance a bowl of chili. Or try Onion Dill Bread with fish, Wild Rice Bread, Cranberry Nut Bread, or Herb Corn Bread with poultry. Everyone has different taste associations depending on past experiences. Homemade bread will bring back those delightful memories as you begin to think about what you will be eating in the days ahead.

Whether you are recalling the aroma and taste of freshly baked bread from a time gone by or you are building memories for those younger than yourself, baking bread in your own home is one of the most satisfying activities you can do. Using the modern conveniences of the bread machine, mixer, or food processor makes it possible and enjoyable. With the least amount of time and effort, bread making will become so much a part of living that soon you, too, will be saying, "I can't remember when I last bought a loaf of bread."

Old-Fashioned Buttermilk White Bread

Buttermilk is often used in baking to give bread a softer crumb. With the added goodness of oats, this classic farmhouse bread is a real taste treat.

Ingredients	Small	Medium	Large
Water	¼ cup + 2 tablespoons	¼ cup + 1 tablespoon	½ cup
Buttermilk	½ cup	¾ cup	1 cup
Vegetable oil	2 tablespoons	3 tablespoons	¼ cup
Salt	1 teaspoon	1 ½ teaspoons	2 teaspoons
Sugar	2 tablespoons	3 tablespoons	¼ cup
Oatmeal	¼ cup	⅓ cup	½ cup
Bread flour	2 ¼ cups	3 cups	4 cups
Active dry yeast	1 ½ teaspoons	2 ¼ teaspoons	1 tablespoon

Bread Machine Method

Have liquid ingredients at 80° F and all others at room temperature. Place ingredients in pan in the order specified in your owner's manual. Select basic cycle and medium/normal crust. Do not use the delay timer.

Mixer Methods

Using ingredient amounts listed for medium loaf, combine yeast, 1 cup flour, and other dry ingredients. Combine liquids and heat to 120° to 130° F.

Hand-Held Mixer Method Combine dry mixture and liquid ingredients in mixing bowl on low speed. Beat 2 to 3 minutes on medium speed. By hand, stir in enough remaining flour to make a firm dough. Knead on floured surface 5 to 7 minutes or until smooth and elastic. Use additional flour if necessary.

Stand Mixer Method Combine dry mixture and liquid ingredients in mixing bowl with paddle or beaters for 4 minutes on medium speed. Gradually add flour and knead with dough hook(s) 5 to 7 minutes until smooth and elastic.

Food Processor Method Put dry mixture in processing bowl with steel blade. While motor is running, add liquid ingredients. Process until mixed. Continue processing, adding remaining flour until dough forms a ball.

Rising, Shaping, and Baking

Place dough in lightly oiled bowl and turn to grease top. Cover; let rise until dough tests ripe. Turn dough onto lightly floured surface; punch down to remove air bubbles. Roll or pat into a 14- x 7-inch rectangle. Starting with shorter side, roll up tightly, pressing dough into roll. Pinch edges and ends to seal. Place in greased 9- x 5-inch loaf pan. Cover; let rise until indentation remains after touching. Bake in preheated 375° F oven 30 to 40 minutes. Remove from pan; cool.

Makes 1 loaf.

Viennese Bread

Along with their pastries, Viennese bakers are world renowned for their classic breads. Viennese bread, with its light crumb and crisp crust, is the perfect dinner loaf.

Ingredients	Small	Medium	Large
Water	1 ¼ cups	1 ¼ cups	1 ½ cups
Salt	1 teaspoon	1 teaspoon	1 ¼ teaspoons
Sugar	1 ½ teaspoons	1 ½ teaspoons	2 teaspoons
White cornmeal	2 tablespoons	3 tablespoons	¼ cup
Bread flour	3 cups	3 ¾ cups	4 ¾ cups
Active dry yeast	2 ¼ teaspoons	2 ¼ teaspoons	1 tablespoon

Bread Machine Method

Have water at 80° F and all other ingredients at room temperature. Place ingredients in pan in the order specified in your owner's manual. Select basic cycle and medium/normal crust.

Mixer Methods

Using ingredient amounts listed for medium loaf, combine yeast, 1 cup flour, and other dry ingredients. Heat water to 120° to 130° F.

Hand-Held Mixer Method Combine dry mixture and water in mixing bowl on low speed. Beat 2 to 3 minutes on medium speed. By hand, stir in enough remaining flour to make a firm dough. Knead on floured surface 5 to 7 minutes or until smooth and elastic. Use additional flour if necessary.

Stand Mixer Method Combine dry mixture and water in mixing bowl with paddle or beaters for 4 minutes on medium speed. Gradually add remaining flour and knead with dough hook(s) 5 to 7 minutes until smooth and elastic.

Food Processor Method Put dry mixture in processing bowl with steel blade. While motor is running, add water. Process until mixed. Continue processing, adding remaining flour until dough forms a ball.

Rising, Shaping, and Baking

Place dough in lightly oiled bowl and turn to grease top. Cover; let rise until dough tests ripe. Turn dough onto lightly floured surface; punch down to remove air bubbles. Roll or pat into a 14- x 7-inch rectangle. Starting with shorter side, roll up tightly, pressing dough into roll. Pinch edges and taper ends to seal. Place on lightly greased cookie sheet sprinkled with cornmeal. Cover; let rise until indentation remains after touching. With very sharp knife, make 2 or 3 diagonal slashes across top of loaf. Brush with cold water. Bake in preheated 425° F oven 30 to 40 minutes. Spray or brush loaf with cold water several times during first 10 minutes of baking for a crisper crust. Remove from cookie sheet; cool.

Makes 1 loaf.

Green Onion Potato Bread

During the days of homesteading, pioneer wives often had to extend their meager supply of wheat by adding other starches to their bread dough as with potato bread. The chopped green onions in our recipe update this American classic.

Ingredients	Small	Medium	Large
Milk	⅓ cup	½ cup + 1 tablespoon	½ cup + 2 tablespoons
Egg(s), room temperature	1	2	2
Vegetable oil	2 tablespoons	3 tablespoons	¼ cup
Baked potato, peeled and mashed	⅓ cup	½ cup	⅔ cup
Chopped green onions, white and green pieces	¼ cup	⅓ cup	½ cup
Salt	1 teaspoon	1 ½ teaspoons	2 teaspoons
Sugar	2 tablespoons	3 tablespoons	¼ cup
Bread flour	2 ¼ cups	3 cups	4 cups
Active dry yeast	1 ½ teaspoons	2 ¼ teaspoons	1 tablespoon

Bread Machine Method

Have liquid ingredients at 80° F and all others at room temperature. Place ingredients in pan in the order specified in your owner's manual. Select basic cycle and medium/normal crust. Do not use the delay timer.

Mixer Methods

Using ingredient amounts listed for medium loaf, combine yeast, 1 cup flour, sugar, and salt. Combine liquids, except eggs, and heat to 120° to 130° F.

Hand-Held Mixer Method Combine dry mixture, liquid ingredients, potato, and onion in mixing bowl on low speed. Beat 2 to 3 minutes on medium speed. Add eggs; beat 1 minute. By hand, stir in enough remaining flour to make a firm dough. Knead on floured surface 5 to 7 minutes or until smooth and elastic. Use additional flour if necessary.

Stand Mixer Method Combine dry mixture, liquid ingredients, potato, and onion in mixing bowl with paddle or beaters for 4 minutes on medium speed. Add eggs; beat 1 minute. Gradually add remaining flour and knead with dough hook(s) 5 to 7 minutes until smooth and elastic.

Food Processor Method Put dry mixture in processing bowl with steel blade. While motor is running, add eggs, liquid ingredients, potato, and onion. Process until mixed. Continue processing, adding remaining flour until dough forms a ball.

Rising, Shaping, and Baking

Place dough in lightly oiled bowl and turn to grease top. Cover; let rise until dough tests ripe. Turn dough onto lightly floured surface; punch down to remove air bubbles. Roll or pat into a 14- x 7-inch rectangle. Starting with shorter side, roll up tightly, pressing dough into roll. Pinch edges and ends to seal. Place in greased 9- x 5-inch loaf pan. Cover; let rise until indentation remains after touching. Bake in preheated 375° F oven 30 to 40 minutes. Remove from pan; cool.

Makes 1 loaf.

Herb Corn Bread

The quintessential bread for making sandwiches with leftover roast chicken or turkey. Herb corn bread is also the perfect choice for making homemade stuffing.

Ingredients	Small	Medium	Large
Water	½ cup	½ cup	½ cup + 2 tablespoons
Evaporated milk	½ cup	¾ cup	1 cup
Vegetable oil	2 tablespoons	3 tablespoons	¼ cup
Dried sweet marjoram	pinch	⅛ teaspoon	¼ teaspoon
Dried ginger	pinch	⅛ teaspoon	¼ teaspoon
Celery seed	¾ teaspoon	1 teaspoon	1 ¼ teaspoons
Dried sage	¾ teaspoon	1 teaspoon	1 ¼ teaspoons
Salt	1 teaspoon	1 ½ teaspoons	2 teaspoons
Sugar	2 tablespoons	3 tablespoons	¼ cup
Yellow cornmeal	¼ cup	⅓ cup	½ cup
Bread flour	2 ¼ cups	3 cups	4 cups
Active dry yeast	1 ½ teaspoons	2 ¼ teaspoons	1 tablespoon

Bread Machine Method

Have liquid ingredients at 80° F and all others at room temperature. Place ingredients in pan in the order specified in your owner's manual. Select basic cycle and medium/normal crust. Do not use the delay timer.

Mixer Methods

Using ingredient amounts listed for medium loaf, combine yeast, 1 cup flour, and other dry ingredients. Combine liquids and heat to 120° to 130° F.

Hand-Held Mixer Method Combine dry mixture and liquid ingredients in mixing bowl on low speed. Beat 2 to 3 minutes on medium speed. By hand, stir in enough remaining flour to make a firm dough. Knead on floured surface 5 to 7 minutes or until smooth and elastic. Use additional flour if necessary.

Stand Mixer Method Combine dry mixture and liquid ingredients in mixing bowl with paddle or beaters for 4 minutes on medium speed. Gradually add remaining flour and knead with dough hook(s) 5 to 7 minutes until smooth and elastic.

Food Processor Method Put dry mixture in processing bowl with steel blade. While motor is running, add liquid ingredients. Process until mixed. Continue processing, adding remaining flour until dough forms a ball.

Rising, Shaping, and Baking

Place dough in lightly oiled bowl and turn to grease top. Cover; let rise until dough tests ripe. Turn dough onto lightly floured surface; punch down to remove air bubbles. Roll or pat into a 14- x 7-inch rectangle. Starting with shorter side, roll up tightly, pressing dough into roll. Pinch edges and ends to seal. Place in greased 9- x 5-inch loaf pan. Cover; let rise until indentation remains after touching. Bake in preheated 375° F oven 30 to 40 minutes. Remove from pan; cool.

Makes 1 loaf.

Jalapeño Cheddar Bread

The perfect blend of spicy Jalapeño peppers, cornmeal, and Cheddar cheese gives this bread its south-of-the-border flavor.

Ingredients	Small	Medium	Large
Water	½ cup	½ cup + 3 tablespoons	¾ cup + 2 tablespoons
Egg, room temperature	1	1	1
Vegetable oil	3 tablespoons	¼ cup	¼ cup + 1 tablespoon
Salt	1 teaspoon	1 ½ teaspoons	2 teaspoons
Sugar	4 teaspoons	2 tablespoons	2 tablespoons + 2 teaspoons
Yellow cornmeal	⅓ cup	½ cup	⅔ cup
Shredded Cheddar cheese	¾ cup	1 cup	1 ¼ cups
Chopped jalapeño peppers	1 tablespoon + 1 ½ teaspoons	2 tablespoons	2 tablespoons + 1 ½ teaspoons
Bread flour	2 ¼ cups	3 cups	4 cups
Active dry yeast	1 ½ teaspoons	2 ¼ teaspoons	1 tablespoon

Bread Machine Method

Have liquid ingredients at 80° F and all others at room temperature. Place ingredients in pan in the order specified in your owner's manual. Select basic cycle and medium/normal crust. Do not use the delay timer.

Mixer Methods

Using ingredient amounts listed for medium loaf, combine yeast, 1 cup flour, and other dry ingredients. Combine liquids, except egg, and heat to 120° to 130° F.

Hand-Held Mixer Method Combine dry mixture and liquid ingredients, except egg, in mixing bowl on low speed. Beat 2 to 3 minutes on medium speed. Add egg; beat 1 minute. By hand, stir in enough remaining flour to make a firm dough. Knead on floured surface 5 to 7 minutes or until smooth and elastic. Use additional flour if necessary.

Stand Mixer Method Combine dry mixture and liquid ingredients, except egg, in mixing bowl with paddle or beaters for 4 minutes on medium speed. Add egg; beat 1 minute. Gradually add remaining flour and knead with dough hook(s) 5 to 7 minutes until smooth and elastic.

Food Processor Method Put dry mixture in processing bowl with steel blade. While motor is running, add liquid ingredients and egg. Process until mixed. Continue processing, adding remaining flour until dough forms a ball.

Rising, Shaping, and Baking

Place dough in lightly oiled bowl and turn to grease top. Cover; let rise until dough tests ripe. Turn dough onto lightly floured surface; punch down to remove air bubbles. Roll or pat into a 14- x 7-inch rectangle. Starting with shorter side, roll up tightly, pressing dough into roll. Pinch edges and ends to seal. Place in greased 9- x 5-inch loaf pan. Cover; let rise until indentation remains after touching. Bake in preheated 375° F oven 30 to 40 minutes. Remove from pan; cool.

Makes 1 loaf.

Hearty Rye Bread

A quick and easy rendition of classic rye bread made with beer for that special sour rye flavor.

Ingredients	Small	Medium	Large
Beer	½ cup	1 cup	1 cup + 2 tablespoons
Vegetable oil	2 tablespoons	3 tablespoons	¼ cup
Caraway seeds	½ teaspoon	1 teaspoon	1 ½ teaspoons
Fennel seeds	¼ teaspoon	½ teaspoon	¾ teaspoon
Orange zest	¼ teaspoon	½ teaspoon	¾ teaspoon
Salt	½ teaspoon	1 teaspoon	1 ½ teaspoons
Brown sugar	2 tablespoons	3 tablespoons	¼ cup
Rye flour	¼ cup	½ cup	1 cup
Bread flour	1 ¾ cups	2 ½ cups	3 cups
Active dry yeast	1 ½ teaspoons	2 ¼ teaspoons	1 tablespoon

Bread Machine Method

Have liquid ingredients at 80° F and all others at room temperature. Place ingredients in pan in the order specified in your owner's manual. Select basic cycle and medium/normal crust.

Mixer Methods

Using ingredient amounts listed for medium loaf, combine yeast, 1 cup bread flour, and other dry ingredients, except rye flour. Combine liquids and heat to 120° to 130° F.

Hand-Held Mixer Method Combine dry mixture and liquid ingredients in mixing bowl on low speed. Beat 2 to 3 minutes on medium speed. By hand, stir in rye flour and enough remaining bread flour to make a firm dough. Knead on floured surface 5 to 7 minutes or until smooth and elastic. Use additional bread flour if necessary.

Stand Mixer Method Combine dry mixture and liquid ingredients in mixing bowl with paddle or beaters for 4 minutes on medium speed. Gradually add rye flour and remaining bread flour and knead with dough hook(s) 5 to 7 minutes until smooth and elastic.

Food Processor Method Put dry mixture in processing bowl with steel blade. While motor is running, add liquid ingredients. Process until mixed. Continue processing, adding rye flour and remaining bread flour until dough forms a ball.

Rising, Shaping, and Baking

Place dough in lightly oiled bowl and turn to grease top. Cover; let rise until dough tests ripe. Turn dough onto lightly floured surface; punch down to remove air bubbles. Roll or pat into a 14- x 7-inch rectangle. Starting with longer side, roll up tightly, pressing dough into roll. Pinch edges and taper ends to seal. Place on lightly greased cookie sheet. Cover; let rise until indentation remains after touching. With very sharp knife, make 2 or 3 diagonal slashes across top of loaf. While dough is rising, place an 8-inch square pan on lowest rack of oven and preheat to 450° F. When the oven reaches 450° F, fill the 8-inch pan with about 2 cups boiling water. Reduce oven temperature to 400° F and place loaf on cookie sheet on rack above water. Bake 40 to 45 minutes. Remove from cookie sheet; cool.

Makes 1 loaf.

Santa Fe Chili Bread

Try serving this bread with a favorite Tex-Mex dish, or use to make grilled Cheddar cheese sandwiches.

Ingredients	Small	Medium	Large
Water	½ cup	½ cup + 1 tablespoon	¾ cup + 2 tablespoons
Fat-free refried beans	¾ cup	1 cup	1 ¼ cups
Vegetable oil	2 tablespoons	3 tablespoons	¼ cup
Yellow cornmeal	⅓ cup	½ cup	⅔ cup
Dried chili powder	1 ½ teaspoons	2 teaspoons	2 ½ teaspoons
Dried onion flakes	1 ½ teaspoons	2 teaspoons	2 ½ teaspoons
Salt	¾ teaspoon	1 teaspoon	1 ¼ teaspoons
Sugar	2 tablespoons	3 tablespoons	¼ cup
Bread flour	2 ¼ cups	3 cups	4 cups
Active dry yeast	1 ½ teaspoons	2 ¼ teaspoons	1 tablespoon

Bread Machine Method

Have liquid ingredients at 80° F and all others at room temperature. Place ingredients in pan in the order specified in your owner's manual. Select basic cycle and medium/normal crust. Do not use the delay timer.

Mixer Methods

Using ingredient amounts listed for medium loaf, combine yeast, 1 cup flour, and other dry ingredients. Combine water, beans, and oil; heat to 120° to 130° F.

Hand-Held Mixer Method Combine dry mixture and liquid ingredients in mixing bowl on low speed. Beat 2 to 3 minutes on medium speed. By hand, stir in enough remaining flour to make a firm dough. Knead on floured surface 5 to 7 minutes or until smooth and elastic. Use additional flour if necessary.

Stand Mixer Method Combine dry mixture and liquid ingredients in mixing bowl with paddle or beaters for 4 minutes on medium speed. Gradually add remaining flour and knead with dough hook(s) 5 to 7 minutes until smooth and elastic.

Food Processor Method Put dry mixture in processing bowl with steel blade. While motor is running, add liquid ingredients. Process until mixed. Continue processing, adding remaining flour until dough forms a ball.

Rising, Shaping, and Baking

Place dough in lightly oiled bowl and turn to grease top. Cover; let rise until dough tests ripe. Turn dough onto lightly floured surface; punch down to remove air bubbles. Roll or pat into a 14- x 7-inch rectangle. Starting with shorter side, roll up tightly, pressing dough into roll. Pinch edges and ends to seal. Place in greased 9- x 5-inch loaf pan. Cover; let rise until indentation remains after touching. Bake in preheated 375° F oven 30 to 40 minutes. Remove from pan; cool.

Makes 1 loaf.

Carrot Raisin Bread

Just like the popular Carrot Raisin Salad, this bread has the subtle tang of mayonnaise combined with the sweetness of carrots and raisins.

Ingredients	Small	Medium	Large
Water	½ cup + 2 tablespoons	¾ cup + 1 tablespoon	1 cup
Mayonnaise	2 tablespoons	3 tablespoons	¼ cup
Grated carrots	⅓ cup	½ cup	⅔ cup
Salt	1 teaspoon	1 ½ teaspoons	2 teaspoons
Sugar	2 tablespoons	3 tablespoons	¼ cup
Bread flour	2 ¼ cups	3 cups	4 cups
Active dry yeast	1 ½ teaspoons	2 ¼ teaspoons	1 tablespoon
Raisins	¼ cup	⅓ cup	½ cup

Bread Machine Method

Have liquid ingredients at 80° F and all others at room temperature. Place ingredients in pan in the order specified in your owner's manual. Select basic cycle and medium/normal crust. Raisins can be added 5 minutes before the end of the last kneading. Do not use the delay timer.

Mixer Methods

Using ingredient amounts listed for medium loaf, combine yeast, 1 cup flour, and other dry ingredients, except raisins. Combine water and mayonnaise; heat to 120° to 130° F.

Hand-Held Mixer Method Combine dry mixture and liquid ingredients in mixing bowl on low speed. Beat 2 to 3 minutes on medium speed. By hand, stir in raisins and enough remaining flour to make a firm dough. Knead on floured surface 5 to 7 minutes or until smooth and elastic. Use additional flour if necessary.

Stand Mixer Method Combine dry mixture and liquid ingredients in mixing bowl with paddle or beaters for 4 minutes on medium speed. Gradually add raisins and remaining flour and knead with dough hook(s) 5 to 7 minutes until smooth and elastic.

Food Processor Method Put dry mixture in processing bowl with steel blade. While motor is running, add liquid ingredients. Process until mixed. Continue processing, adding remaining flour until dough forms a ball. Add raisins; pulse just until mixed.

Rising, Shaping, and Baking

Place dough in lightly oiled bowl and turn to grease top. Cover; let rise until dough tests ripe. Turn dough onto lightly floured surface; punch down to remove air bubbles. Roll or pat into a 14- x 7-inch rectangle. Starting with shorter side, roll up tightly, pressing dough into roll. Pinch edges and ends to seal. Place in greased 9- x 5-inch loaf pan. Cover; let rise until indentation remains after touching. Bake in preheated 375° F oven 30 to 40 minutes. Remove from pan; cool.

Makes 1 loaf.

Cranberry-Nut Bread

This delicious sweet bread is chock-full of nuts and dried, sweetened cranberries, making it the perfect bread for a holiday breakfast, or for that matter, any time of the year.

Ingredients	Small	Medium	Large
Water	2 tablespoons	2 tablespoons	5 tablespoons
Milk	⅓ cup	½ cup	½ cup
Egg(s), room temperature	1	2	2
Vegetable oil	2 tablespoons	3 tablespoons	¼ cup
Orange zest	1 ½ teaspoons	2 teaspoons	2 ½ teaspoons
Almond extract	1 teaspoon	1 ½ teaspoons	2 teaspoons
Salt	1 teaspoon	1 ½ teaspoons	2 teaspoons
Sugar	2 tablespoons	3 tablespoons	¼ cup
Whole wheat flour	½ cup	1 cup	1 ½ cups
Bread flour	1 ¾ cups	2 cups	2 ½ cups
Active dry yeast	1 ½ teaspoons	2 ¼ teaspoons	1 tablespoon
Dried cranberries	⅓ cup	½ cup	⅔ cup
Slivered almonds	¼ cup	⅓ cup	½ cup

Bread Machine Method

Have liquid ingredients at 80° F and all others at room temperature. Place ingredients in pan in the order specified in your owner's manual. Select basic cycle and medium/normal crust. Cranberries and almonds can be added 5 minutes before the end of the last kneading. Do not use the delay timer.

Mixer Methods

Using ingredient amounts listed for medium loaf, combine yeast, 1 cup bread flour, and other dry ingredients, except whole wheat flour, cranberries, and almonds. Combine liquids, except eggs, and heat to 120° to 130° F.

Hand-Held Mixer Method Combine dry mixture and liquid ingredients in mixing bowl on low speed. Beat 2 to 3 minutes on medium speed. Add eggs; beat 1 minute. By hand, stir in whole wheat flour, cranberries, almonds, and enough remaining bread flour to make a firm dough. Knead on floured surface 5 to 7 minutes or until smooth and elastic. Use additional flour if necessary.

Stand Mixer Method Combine dry mixture and liquid ingredients in mixing bowl with paddle or beaters for 4 minutes on medium speed. Add eggs; beat 1 minute. Gradually add whole wheat flour, cranberries, almonds, and remaining bread flour and knead with dough hook(s) 5 to 7 minutes or until smooth and elastic.

Food Processor Method Put dry mixture in processing bowl with steel blade. While motor is running, add eggs and liquid ingredients. Process until mixed. Continue processing, adding whole wheat flour and remaining bread flour until dough forms a ball. Add cranberries and almonds; pulse just until mixed.

Rising, Shaping, and Baking

Place dough in lightly oiled bowl and turn to grease top. Cover; let rise until dough tests ripe. Turn dough onto lightly floured surface; punch down to remove air bubbles. Roll or pat into a 14- x 7-inch rectangle. Starting with shorter side, roll up tightly. Pinch edges and ends to seal. Place in greased 9- x 5-inch loaf pan. Cover; let rise until indentation remains after touching. Bake in preheated 375° F oven 30 to 40 minutes. Remove from pan; cool.

Makes 1 loaf.

Cream of Orange Bread

The sunny flavor of orange shines through with every slice of this wonderful bread.

Ingredients	Small	Medium	Large
Water	2 tablespoons	2 tablespoons	½ cup
Orange juice	3 tablespoons	¼ cup	¼ cup + 1 tablespoon
Milk	½ cup	⅔ cup	¾ cup
Butter, room temperature	2 tablespoons	3 tablespoons	¼ cup
Dried ginger	pinch	⅛ teaspoon	¼ teaspoon
Lemon zest	1 teaspoon	1 teaspoon	1 teaspoon
Orange zest	1 tablespoon	2 tablespoons	3 tablespoons
Salt	½ teaspoon	¾ teaspoon	1 teaspoon
Sugar	2 tablespoons	3 tablespoons	¼ cup
Bread flour	2 ¼ cups	3 cups	4 cups
Active dry yeast	1 ½ teaspoons	2 ¼ teaspoons	1 tablespoon

Bread Machine Method

Have liquid ingredients at 80° F and all others at room temperature. Place ingredients in pan in the order specified in your owner's manual. Select basic cycle and medium/normal crust. Do not use the delay timer.

Mixer Methods

Using ingredient amounts listed for medium loaf, combine yeast, 1 cup flour, and other dry ingredients. Combine water, orange juice, and milk; heat to 120° to 130° F.

Hand-Held Mixer Method Combine dry mixture, liquid ingredients, and butter in mixing bowl on low speed. Beat 2 to 3 minutes on medium speed. By hand, stir in enough remaining flour to make a firm dough. Knead on floured surface 5 to 7 minutes or until smooth and elastic. Use additional flour if necessary.

Stand Mixer Method Combine dry mixture, liquid ingredients, and butter in mixing bowl with paddle or beaters for 4 minutes on medium speed. Gradually add remaining flour and knead with dough hook(s) 5 to 7 minutes until smooth and elastic.

Food Processor Method Put dry mixture in processing bowl with steel blade. While motor is running, add butter and liquid ingredients. Process until mixed. Continue processing, adding remaining flour until dough forms a ball.

Rising, Shaping, and Baking

Place dough in lightly oiled bowl and turn to grease top. Cover; let rise until dough tests ripe. Turn dough onto lightly floured surface; punch down to remove air bubbles. Roll or pat into a 14- x 7-inch rectangle. Starting with shorter side, roll up tightly, pressing dough into roll. Pinch edges and ends to seal. Place in greased 9- x 5-inch loaf pan. Cover; let rise until indentation remains after touching. Bake in preheated 375° F oven 30 to 40 minutes. Remove from pan; cool.

Makes 1 loaf.

Spiced Pumpkin Bread

Perfect at breakfast or served as a low-fat dessert, this bread is rich in beta carotene.

Ingredients	Small	Medium	Large
Water	¼ cup + 1 tablespoon	1 tablespoon	¼ cup
Pumpkin, canned	⅔ cup	1 cup	1 ⅓ cups
Vegetable oil	2 tablespoons	3 tablespoons	¼ cup
Egg(s), room temperature	1	2	2
Ground cloves	¼ teaspoon	¼ teaspoon	¼ teaspoon
Ground nutmeg	½ teaspoon	½ teaspoon	½ teaspoon
Dried ginger	¼ teaspoon	½ teaspoon	½ teaspoon
Ground cinnamon	1 ½ teaspoons	2 teaspoons	2 ½ teaspoons
Salt	1 teaspoon	1 ½ teaspoons	2 teaspoons
Brown sugar	2 tablespoons	¼ cup	¼ cup + 2 tablespoons
Bread flour	2 ¼ cups	3 cups	4 cups
Active dry yeast	1 ½ teaspoons	2 ¼ teaspoons	1 tablespoon
Pecan halves	⅓ cup	½ cup	⅔ cup

Bread Machine Method

Have liquid ingredients at 80° F and all others at room temperature. Place ingredients in pan in the order specified in your owner's manual. Add pecans 5 minutes before end of kneading. Select basic cycle and medium/normal crust. Do not use the delay timer.

Mixer Methods

Using ingredient amounts listed for medium loaf, combine yeast, 1 cup flour, and other dry ingredients, except pecans. Combine liquids, except eggs; heat to 120° to 130° F.

Hand Held Mixer Method Combine dry mixture and liquid ingredients in mixing bowl on low speed. Beat 2 to 3 minutes on medium speed. Add eggs; beat 1 minute. By hand, stir in pecans and enough remaining flour to make a firm dough. Knead on floured surface 5 to 7 minutes or until smooth and elastic. Use additional flour if necessary.

Stand Mixer Method Combine dry mixture and liquid ingredients in mixing bowl with paddle or beaters for 4 minutes on medium speed. Add eggs; beat 1 minute. Gradually add pecans and remaining flour and knead with dough hook(s) 5 to 7 minutes until smooth and elastic.

Food Processor Method Put dry mixture in processing bowl with steel blade. While motor is running, add eggs and liquid ingredients. Process until mixed. Continue processing, adding remaining flour until dough forms a ball. Add pecans; pulse just until mixed.

Rising, Shaping, and Baking

Place dough in lightly oiled bowl and turn to grease top. Cover; let rise until dough tests ripe. Turn dough onto lightly floured surface; punch down to remove air bubbles. Roll or pat into a 14- x 7-inch rectangle. Starting with shorter side, roll up tightly, pressing dough into roll. Pinch edges and ends to seal. Place in greased 9- x 5-inch loaf pan. Cover; let rise until indentation remains after touching. Bake in preheated 375° F oven 30 to 40 minutes. Remove from pan; cool.

Makes 1 loaf.

Onion Dill Bread

Try serving this all time favorite sliced thin and toasted with a pat of sweet butter and a piece of smoked salmon.

Ingredients	Small	Medium	Large
Water	3 tablespoons	2 tablespoons	¼ cup
Plain yogurt	½ cup	¾ cup	1 cup
Vegetable oil	1 tablespoon	1 tablespoon + 1 teaspoon	1 tablespoon + 2 teaspoons
Egg, room temperature	1	1	1
Dill weed	1 ½ teaspoons	2 teaspoons	2 ½ teaspoons
Dried minced onions	2 teaspoons	1 tablespoon	1 tablespoon + 1 teaspoon
Salt	1 teaspoon	1 ½ teaspoons	2 teaspoons
Sugar	1 tablespoon + 1 teaspoon	2 tablespoons	2 tablespoons + 2 teaspoons
Bread flour	2 ¼ cups	3 cups	4 cups
Active dry yeast	1 ½ teaspoons	2 ¼ teaspoons	1 tablespoon

Bread Machine Method

Have liquid ingredients at 80° F and all others at room temperature. Place ingredients in pan in the order specified in your owner's manual. Select basic cycle and medium/normal crust. Do not use the delay timer.

Mixer Methods

Using ingredient amounts listed for medium loaf, combine yeast, 1 cup flour, and other dry ingredients. Combine water, yogurt, and oil; heat to 120° to 130° F.

Hand-Held Mixer Method Combine dry mixture and liquid ingredients in mixing bowl on low speed. Beat 2 to 3 minutes on medium speed. Add egg; beat 1 minute. By hand, stir in enough remaining flour to make a firm dough. Knead on floured surface 5 to 7 minutes or until smooth and elastic. Use additional flour if necessary.

Stand Mixer Method Combine dry mixture and liquid ingredients in mixing bowl with paddle or beaters for 4 minutes on medium speed. Add egg; beat 1 minute. Gradually add remaining flour and knead with dough hook(s) 5 to 7 minutes until smooth and elastic.

Food Processor Method Put dry mixture in processing bowl with steel blade. While motor is running, add egg and liquid ingredients. Process until mixed. Continue processing, adding remaining flour until dough forms a ball.

Rising, Shaping, and Baking

Place dough in lightly oiled bowl and turn to grease top. Cover; let rise until dough tests ripe. Turn dough onto lightly floured surface; punch down to remove air bubbles. Roll or pat into a 14- x 7-inch rectangle. Starting with shorter side, roll up tightly, pressing dough into roll. Pinch edges and ends to seal. Place in greased 9- x 5-inch loaf pan. Cover; let rise until indentation remains after touching. Bake in preheated 375° F oven 30 to 40 minutes. Remove from pan; cool.

Makes 1 loaf.

Dough Preparation

Left: Bread machine dough as it should look after 3 to 5 minutes of kneading.

Below: Performing the "Ripe Test."

Above: "Ripe" dough, ready to punch down.

Right: Dough "ripe" and ready for the oven.

Focaccia

Clockwise, starting in upper right:
Green Onion Potato Bread, Pumpkin Bread, San
Francisco Sourdough Bread, Special Whole Wheat
Bread, Vienesse Bread, Apple Cinnamon Raisin

Herb Corn Bread

Clockwise from lower left: Oatmeal Walnut
Bread, New York Bagels, Refrigerator Rolls,
Old-fashioned Buttermilk White Bread

Apple Cinnamon Raisin Bread

Apple juice, cinnamon, and raisins—a subtle blend of flavors, a marvelous loaf of bread!

Ingredients	Small	Medium	Large
Water	¼ cup	¼ cup + 1 tablespoon	¼ cup
Apple juice	½ cup	¾ cup	1 cup
Vegetable oil	2 teaspoons	1 tablespoon	1 tablespoon + 2 teaspoons
Salt	¾ teaspoon	1 teaspoon	1 ¼ teaspoons
Sugar	2 teaspoons	1 tablespoon	1 tablespoon + 2 teaspoons
Ground cinnamon	2 teaspoons	1 tablespoon	1 tablespoon + 1 teaspoon
Bread flour	2 ¼ cups	3 cups	4 cups
Active dry yeast	1 ½ teaspoons	2 ¼ teaspoons	1 tablespoon
Raisins	½ cup	¾ cup	1 cup

Bread Machine Method

Have liquid ingredients at 80° F and all others at room temperature. Place ingredients in pan in the order specified in your owner's manual. Select basic cycle and medium/normal crust. Raisins can be added 5 minutes before the end of the last kneading. Do not use the delay timer.

Mixer Methods

Using ingredient amounts listed for medium loaf, combine yeast, 1 cup flour, and other dry ingredients, except raisins. Combine liquids and heat to 120° to 130° F.

Hand-Held Mixer Method Combine dry mixture and liquid ingredients in mixing bowl on low speed. Beat 2 to 3 minutes on medium speed. By hand, stir in raisins and enough remaining flour to make a firm dough. Knead on floured surface 5 to 7 minutes or until smooth and elastic. Use additional flour if necessary.

Stand Mixer Method Combine dry mixture and liquid ingredients in mixing bowl with paddle or beaters for 4 minutes on medium speed. Gradually add raisins and remaining flour and knead with dough hook(s) 5 to 7 minutes until smooth and elastic.

Food Processor Method Put dry mixture in processing bowl with steel blade. While motor is running, add liquid ingredients. Process until mixed. Continue processing, adding remaining flour until dough forms a ball. Add raisins; pulse just until mixed.

Rising, Shaping, and Baking

Place dough in lightly oiled bowl and turn to grease top. Cover; let rise until dough tests ripe. Turn dough onto lightly floured surface; punch down to remove air bubbles. Roll or pat into a 14- x 7-inch rectangle. Starting with shorter side, roll up tightly, pressing dough into roll. Pinch edges and ends to seal. Place in greased 9- x 5-inch loaf pan. Cover; let rise until indentation remains after touching. Bake in preheated 375° F oven 30 to 40 minutes. Remove from pan; cool.

Makes 1 loaf.

Wild Rice Bread

A long-grain marsh grass, wild rice is native to the northern Great Lakes area. In the following Baker's Collection recipe from Eileen Sugar, of Duluth, Minnesota, the wild rice adds a luxurious, nutty flavor and chewy texture to the bread.

Ingredients	Small	Medium	Large
Milk	½ cup + 2 tablespoons	¾ cup + 1 tablespoon	1 ¼ cups
Vegetable oil	1 tablespoon	2 tablespoons	3 tablespoons
Honey	1 tablespoon	2 tablespoons	3 tablespoons
Molasses	2 teaspoons	1 tablespoon	1 tablespoon + 1 teaspoon
Cooked wild rice	1 cup	1 ½ cups	2 cups
Salt	½ teaspoon	1 teaspoon	1 ½ teaspoons
Brown sugar	1 tablespoon	2 tablespoons	3 tablespoons
Bread flour	2 cups	3 cups	4 cups
Active dry yeast	1 ½ teaspoons	2 ¼ teaspoons	1 tablespoon

Bread Machine Method

Have liquid ingredients at 80° F and all others at room temperature. Place ingredients in pan in the order specified in your owner's manual. Select basic cycle and medium/normal crust.

Mixer Methods

Using ingredient amounts listed for medium loaf, combine yeast, 1 cup flour, and other dry ingredients. Combine liquids and heat to 120° to 130° F.

Hand-Held Mixer Method Combine rice, dry mixture, and liquid ingredients in mixing bowl on low speed. Beat 2 to 3 minutes on medium speed. By hand, stir in enough remaining flour to make a firm dough. Knead on floured surface 5 to 7 minutes or until smooth and elastic. Use additional flour if necessary.

Stand Mixer Method Combine rice, dry mixture, and liquid ingredients in mixing bowl with paddle or beaters for 4 minutes on medium speed. Gradually add remaining flour and knead with dough hook(s) 5 to 7 minutes until smooth and elastic.

Food Processor Method Put rice and dry mixture in processing bowl with steel blade. While motor is running, add liquid ingredients. Process until mixed. Continue processing, adding remaining flour until dough forms a ball.

Rising, Shaping, and Baking

Place dough in lightly oiled bowl and turn to grease top. Cover; let rise until dough tests ripe. Turn dough onto lightly floured surface; punch down to remove air bubbles. Roll or pat into a 14- x 7-inch rectangle. Starting with shorter side, roll up tightly, pressing dough into roll. Pinch edges and ends to seal. Place in greased 9- x 5-inch loaf pan. Cover; let rise until indentation remains after touching. Bake in preheated 375° F oven 30 to 40 minutes. Remove from pan; cool.

Makes 1 loaf.

Buttermilk Whole Wheat Raisin Bread

This bread combines many of our favorite ingredients in one loaf. Buttermilk for a soft crumb, whole wheat flour for added fiber, and plump raisins for sweetness.

Ingredients	Small	Medium	Large
Water	¾ cup + 1 tablespoon	1 cup	1 cup + 2 tablespoons
Vegetable oil	1 tablespoon	2 tablespoons	3 tablespoons
Buttermilk powder	2 tablespoons	3 tablespoons	¼ cup
Salt	1 teaspoon	1 ½ teaspoons	2 teaspoons
Brown Sugar	2 tablespoons	3 tablespoons	¼ cup
Whole Wheat flour	1 ½ cups	2 cups	2 ½ cups
Bread flour	¾ cup	1 cup	1 ½ cups
Active dry yeast	2 ¼ teaspoons	1 tablespoon	1 tablespoon + 1 ½ teaspoons
Raisins	⅓ cup	½ cup	⅔ cup

Bread Machine Method

Have liquid ingredients at 80° F and all others at room temperature. Place ingredients in pan in the order specified in your owner's manual. Select basic cycle and medium/normal crust. Raisins can be added 5 minutes before the end of the last kneading.

Mixer Methods

Using ingredient amounts listed for medium loaf, combine yeast, 1 cup bread flour, and other dry ingredients, except whole wheat flour and raisins. Combine liquids and heat to 120° to 130° F.

Hand-Held Mixer Method Combine dry mixture and liquid ingredients in mixing bowl on low speed. Beat 2 to 3 minutes on medium speed. By hand, stir in whole wheat flour, raisins, and enough remaining bread flour to make a firm dough. Knead on floured surface 5 to 7 minutes or until smooth and elastic. Use additional flour if necessary.

Stand Mixer Method Combine dry mixture and liquid ingredients in mixing bowl with paddle or beaters for 4 minutes on medium speed. Gradually add whole wheat flour, raisins, and remaining bread flour and knead with dough hook(s) 5 to 7 minutes until smooth and elastic.

Food Processor Method Put dry mixture in processing bowl with steel blade. While motor is running, add liquid ingredients. Process until mixed. Continue processing, adding whole wheat flour and remaining bread flour until dough forms a ball. Add raisins; pulse just until mixed.

Rising, Shaping, and Baking

Place dough in lightly oiled bowl and turn to grease top. Cover; let rise until dough tests ripe. Turn dough onto lightly floured surface; punch down to remove air bubbles. Roll or pat into a 14- x 7-inch rectangle. Starting with shorter side, roll up tightly, pressing dough into roll. Pinch edges and ends to seal. Place in greased 9- x 5-inch loaf pan. Cover; let rise until indentation remains after touching. Bake in preheated 375° F oven 30 to 40 minutes. Remove from pan; cool.

Makes 1 loaf.

Everything Bread

Everything Bread from Phyllis Eisenstadt of Brooklyn, New York, is another favorite from our Baker's Collection.

Ingredients	Small	Medium	Large
Water	¾ cup + 3 tablespoons	1 ½ cups + 1 tablespoon	1 ½ cups + 3 tablespoons
Vegetable oil	2 teaspoons	1 tablespoon	1 tablespoon + 2 teaspoons
Salt	1 ½ teaspoons	2 teaspoons	2 ½ teaspoons
Black pepper	¼ teaspoon	½ teaspoon	¾ teaspoon
Dried minced garlic	2 teaspoons	1 tablespoon	1 tablespoon + 2 teaspoons
Dried minced onion	1 tablespoon + 1 ½ teaspoons	2 tablespoons	2 tablespoons + 1 ½ teaspoons
Poppy seeds	1 tablespoon + 1 ½ teaspoons	2 tablespoons	2 tablespoons + 1 ½ teaspoons
Sesame seeds	1 tablespoon + 1 ½ teaspoons	2 tablespoons	2 tablespoons + 1 ½ teaspoons
Caraway seeds	2 teaspoons	1 tablespoon	1 tablespoon + 2 teaspoons
Oatmeal	½ cup	1 cup	1 ½ cups
Bread flour	2 ¼ cups	3 cups	4 cups
Active dry yeast	1 ½ teaspoons	2 ¼ teaspoons	1 tablespoon

Topping

Kosher salt	¾ teaspoon	**Dried minced garlic**	½ teaspoon
Poppy seeds	¾ teaspoon	**Sesame seeds**	¾ teaspoon
Black pepper	pinch	**Dried minced onion**	¾ teaspoon
Caraway seeds	½ teaspoon		

Bread Machine Method

Have liquid ingredients at 80° F and all others at room temperature. Place ingredients in pan in the order specified in your owner's manual. Select basic cycle and medium/normal crust. When machine begins bake cycle, brush top of bread with 1 ½ teaspoons water combined with ⅛ teaspoon cornstarch. Sprinkle with topping. Do not use delay cycle.

Mixer Methods Using ingredient amounts listed for medium loaf, combine yeast, 1 cup flour, and other dry ingredients. Combine liquids and heat to 120° to 130° F.

Hand-Held Mixer Method Combine dry mixture and liquid ingredients in mixing bowl on low speed. Beat 2 to 3 minutes on medium speed. By hand, stir in enough remaining flour to make a firm dough. Knead on floured surface 5 to 7 minutes or until smooth and elastic. Use additional flour if necessary.

Stand Mixer Method Combine dry mixture and liquid ingredients in mixing bowl with paddle or beaters for 4 minutes on medium speed. Gradually add remaining flour and knead with dough hook(s) 5 to 7 minutes until smooth and elastic.

Food Processor Method Put dry mixture in processing bowl with steel blade. While motor is running, add liquid ingredients. Process until mixed. Continue processing, adding remaining flour until dough forms a ball.

Rising, Shaping, and Baking

Place dough in lightly oiled bowl and turn to grease top. Cover; let rise until dough tests ripe. Turn dough onto lightly floured surface; punch down to remove air bubbles. Shape dough into a round loaf. Place on greased cookie sheet. Cover; let rise until indentation remains after touching. Combine 1 ½ teaspoons water and ⅛ teaspoon cornstarch; brush on top. Sprinkle with topping. Bake in preheated 375° F oven 30 to 40 minutes or until tested done. Remove from cookie sheet; cool.

Makes 1 loaf.

Chapter 3
Loaves from Whole Grains

Take good care of yourself, you belong to me, is a just a line from a song, but it is exactly what you will be doing as you enjoy the textures and flavors of wholesome breads. Imagine having toasted Oatmeal Breakfast Bread in the morning, a sandwich of Four-Grain Bread stacked with lettuce, alfalfa sprouts, and tomato for lunch, or a slice of Cracked Wheat Bread with a bowl of hearty soup for dinner. The added whole grains in these breads will not only give your body the fiber, vitamins, and minerals it needs, but will also be an appetizing treat for your taste buds.

If you follow the directions in the section, Storing Dough and Bread, you will be able to have a slice of bread ready to eat in just moments. These breads all freeze well. When they are sliced before freezing, the sections separate easily and are convenient for popping in the toaster, preparing a sandwich, or having with a meal.

Alpine Wheat Bread

This dense, hearty loaf gets its inspiration from that wonderful, whole-grain, Swiss cereal, muesli.

Ingredients	Medium	Large
Water	¾ cup + 3 tablespoons	1 cup
Vegetable oil	3 tablespoons	¼ cup
Molasses	3 tablespoons	¼ cup
Lemon juice	1 ½ teaspoons	2 teaspoons
Egg white(s)	1	2
Ground cinnamon	1 ½ teaspoons	2 teaspoons
Salt	1 ½ teaspoons	2 teaspoons
Whole wheat flour	3 cups	4 cups
Active dry yeast	3 ½ teaspoons	1 tablespoon + 1 ½ teaspoons
Walnuts	½ cup	⅔ cup
Raisins	½ cup	⅔ cup

Cook's Note: Due to the low volume of this loaf, the medium recipe can be used in a small machine.

Bread Machine Method

Have liquid ingredients at 80° F and all others at room temperature. Place ingredients in pan in the order specified in your owner's manual. Select basic cycle and medium/normal crust. Walnuts and raisins can be added 5 minutes before the end of the last kneading. Do not use the delay timer.

Mixer Methods

Using ingredient amounts listed for medium loaf, combine yeast, 1 cup whole wheat flour, and other dry ingredients, except walnuts and raisins. Combine liquids, except egg white, and heat to 120° to 130° F.

Hand-Held Mixer Method Combine dry mixture and liquid ingredients in mixing bowl on low speed. Beat 2 to 3 minutes on medium speed. Add egg white; beat 1 minute. By hand, stir in walnuts, raisins, and enough remaining flour to make a firm dough. Knead on floured surface 5 to 7 minutes or until smooth and elastic. Use additional flour if necessary.

Stand Mixer Method Combine dry mixture and liquid ingredients in mixing bowl with paddle or beaters for 4 minutes on medium speed. Add egg white; beat 1 minute. Gradually add walnuts, raisins, and remaining flour and knead with dough hook(s) 5 to 7 minutes until smooth and elastic.

Food Processor Method Put dry mixture in processing bowl with steel blade. While motor is running, add liquid ingredients, including egg white. Process until mixed. Continue processing, adding remaining flour until dough forms a ball. Add walnuts and raisins; pulse just until mixed.

Rising, Shaping, and Baking

Place dough in lightly oiled bowl and turn to grease top. Cover; let rise until dough tests ripe. Turn dough onto lightly floured surface; punch down to remove air bubbles. Roll or pat into a 14- x 7-inch rectangle. Starting with shorter side, roll up tightly. Pinch edges and ends to seal. Place in greased 9- x 5-inch loaf pan. Cover; let rise until indentation remains after touching. Bake in preheated 375° F oven 30 to 40 minutes. Remove from pan; cool.

Makes 1 loaf.

Oatmeal Walnut Bread

People of Scottish heritage have always highly regarded the use of oats in their baked goods. It is evident in this mellow, whole-grain loaf that the early immigrants brought to the New World.

Ingredients	Small	Medium	Large
Water	½ cup + 1 tablespoon	1 cup	1 ¼ cups + 2 tablespoons
Vegetable oil	1 tablespoon	2 tablespoons	3 tablespoons
Molasses	3 tablespoons	4 tablespoons	5 tablespoons
Salt	1 teaspoon	1 ½ teaspoons	2 teaspoons
Oatmeal	⅓ cup	½ cup	⅔ cup
Whole wheat flour	⅔ cup	1 cup	1 ⅓ cups
Bread flour	1 ⅓ cups	2 cups	2 ⅔ cups
Active dry yeast	1 ½ teaspoons	2 ¼ teaspoons	1 tablespoon
Walnuts	½ cup	¾ cup	1 cup

Bread Machine Method

Have liquid ingredients at 80° F and all others at room temperature. Place ingredients in pan in the order specified in your owner's manual. Select basic cycle and medium/normal crust. Walnuts can be added 5 minutes before the end of the last kneading cycle.

Mixer Methods

Using ingredient amounts listed for medium loaf, combine yeast, 1 cup bread flour, and other dry ingredients, except whole wheat flour and walnuts. Combine liquids and heat to 120° to 130° F.

Hand-Held Mixer Method Combine dry mixture and liquid ingredients in mixing bowl on low speed. Beat 2 to 3 minutes on medium speed. By hand, stir in whole wheat flour, walnuts, and enough remaining bread flour to make a firm dough. Knead on floured surface 5 to 7 minutes or until smooth and elastic. Use additional flour if necessary.

Stand Mixer Method Combine dry mixture and liquid ingredients in mixing bowl with paddle or beaters for 4 minutes on medium speed. Gradually add whole wheat flour, walnuts, and remaining bread flour and knead with dough hook(s) 5 to 7 minutes until smooth and elastic.

Food Processor Method Put dry mixture in processing bowl with steel blade. While motor is running, add liquid ingredients. Process until mixed. Continue processing, adding whole wheat flour and remaining bread flour until dough forms a ball. Add walnuts; pulse just until mixed.

Rising, Shaping, and Baking

Place dough in lightly oiled bowl and turn to grease top. Cover; let rise until dough tests ripe. Turn dough onto lightly floured surface; punch down to remove air bubbles. Shape into a round loaf. Place on greased cookie sheet. Cover; let rise in warm place until indentation remains after touching. Combine 1 egg and 1 tablespoon water; brush top of loaf. Sprinkle with oatmeal. Bake in preheated 375° F oven 30 to 40 minutes. Remove from cookie sheet; cool.

Makes 1 loaf.

Cracked Wheat Bread

The nutritional buzz word for better health is fiber. Besides adding flavor and texture to bread, cracked wheat also adds incredible nutritional value.

Ingredients	Small	Medium	Large
Water	¾ cup + 2 tablespoons	1 ¼ cups + 1 tablespoon	1 ¾ cups
Cracked wheat	½ cup	¾ cup	1 cup
Vegetable oil	1 tablespoon + 1 teaspoon	2 tablespoons	2 tablespoons + 2 teaspoons
Salt	1 teaspoon	1 ½ teaspoons	2 teaspoons
Sugar	1 tablespoon + 1 teaspoon	2 tablespoons	2 tablespoons + 2 teaspoons
Bread flour	2 ¼ cups	3 cups	4 cups
Active dry yeast	1 ½ teaspoons	2 ¼ teaspoons	1 tablespoon

Cook's Note: Bring water to a boil. Place cracked wheat in small mixing bowl and pour water over it; stir. Before using, cool to 80° F for bread machine method and 120° to 130° F for mixer methods.

Bread Machine Method

Have cracked wheat mixture at 80° F and all other ingredients at room temperature. Place ingredients in pan in the order specified in your owner's manual. Select basic cycle and medium/normal crust. Do not use the delay timer.

Mixer Methods

Using ingredient amounts listed for medium loaf, combine yeast, 1 cup flour, and other dry ingredients.

Hand-Held Mixer Method Combine dry mixture with cracked wheat mixture and vegetable oil in mixing bowl on low speed. Beat 2 to 3 minutes on medium speed. By hand, stir in enough remaining flour to make a firm dough. Knead on floured surface 5 to 7 minutes or until smooth and elastic. Use additional flour if necessary.

Stand Mixer Method Combine dry mixture with cracked wheat mixture and vegetable oil in mixing bowl with paddle or beaters for 4 minutes on medium speed. Gradually add remaining flour and knead with dough hook(s) 5 to 7 minutes until smooth.

Food Processor Method Put dry mixture in processing bowl with steel blade. While motor is running, add cracked wheat mixture and vegetable oil. Process until mixed. Continue processing, adding remaining flour until dough forms a ball.

Rising, Shaping, and Baking

Place dough in lightly oiled bowl and turn to grease top. Cover; let rise until dough tests ripe. Turn dough onto lightly floured surface; punch down to remove air bubbles. Roll or pat into a 14- x 7-inch rectangle. Starting with shorter side, roll up tightly, pressing dough into roll. Pinch edges and ends to seal. Place in greased 9- x 5-inch loaf pan. Cover; let rise until indentation remains after touching. Bake in preheated 375° F oven 30 to 40 minutes. Remove from pan; cool.

Makes 1 loaf.

Special Whole Wheat Bread

This bread has a moist, soft crumb and additional protein from cottage cheese.

Ingredients	Medium	Large
Water	3 tablespoons	¼ cup
Milk	¾ cup	1 cup
Cottage cheese	¼ cup	¼ cup + 1 tablespoon
Honey	2 tablespoons	2 tablespoons + 2 teaspoons
Salt	1 ½ teaspoons	2 teaspoons
Whole wheat flour	1 cup	1 ⅓ cups
Bread flour	2 cups	2 ⅔ cups
Active dry yeast	2 ¼ teaspoons	1 tablespoon

Cook's Note: Due to the low volume of this loaf, the medium recipe can be used in a small machine.

Bread Machine Method

Have liquid ingredients at 80° F and all others at room temperature. Place ingredients in pan in the order specified in your owner's manual. Select basic cycle and medium/normal crust. Do not use the delay timer.

Mixer Methods

Using ingredient amounts listed for medium loaf, combine yeast, 1 cup bread flour, and salt. Combine liquids, including cottage cheese, and heat to 120° to 130° F.

Hand-Held Mixer Method Combine dry mixture and liquid ingredients in mixing bowl on low speed. Beat 2 to 3 minutes on medium speed. By hand, stir in whole wheat flour and enough remaining bread flour to make a firm dough. Knead on floured surface 5 to 7 minutes or until smooth and elastic. Use additional flour if necessary.

Stand Mixer Method Combine dry mixture and liquid ingredients in mixing bowl with paddle or beaters for 4 minutes on medium speed. Gradually add whole wheat flour and remaining bread flour and knead with dough hook(s) 5 to 7 minutes until smooth and elastic.

Food Processor Method Put dry mixture in processing bowl with steel blade. While motor is running, add liquid ingredients. Process until mixed. Continue processing, adding whole wheat flour and remaining bread flour until dough forms a ball.

Rising, Shaping, and Baking

Place dough in lightly oiled bowl and turn to grease top. Cover; let rise until dough tests ripe. Turn dough onto lightly floured surface; punch down to remove air bubbles. Roll or pat into a 14- x 7-inch rectangle. Starting with shorter side, roll up tightly, pressing dough into roll. Pinch edges and ends to seal. Place in greased 9- x 5-inch loaf pan. Cover; let rise until indentation remains after touching. Bake in preheated 375° F oven 30 to 40 minutes. Remove from pan; cool.

Makes 1 loaf.

This powerhouse loaf, chock-full of grain and fiber, will satisfy a hungry appetite.

Ingredients	Small	Medium	Large
Water	½ cup + 1 tablespoon	1 cup + 1 tablespoon	1 ¼ cups
Vegetable oil	1 tablespoon	2 tablespoons	3 tablespoons
Molasses	3 tablespoons	4 tablespoons	5 tablespoons
Buttermilk powder	2 tablespoons	3 tablespoons	¼ cup
Oatmeal	3 tablespoons	¼ cup	¼ cup + 1 tablespoon
Yellow cornmeal	3 tablespoons	¼ cup	¼ cup + 1 tablespoon
Salt	1 teaspoon	1 ½ teaspoons	2 teaspoons
Rye flour	3 tablespoons	¼ cup	¼ cup + 1 tablespoon
Whole wheat flour	⅓ cup	½ cup	⅔ cup
Bread flour	1 cup	2 cups	3 cups
Active dry yeast	1 ½ teaspoons	2 ¼ teaspoons	1 tablespoon

Bread Machine Method

Have liquid ingredients at 80° F and all others at room temperature. Place ingredients in pan in the order specified in your owner's manual. Select basic cycle and medium/normal crust.

Mixer Methods

Using ingredient amounts listed for medium loaf, combine yeast, 1 cup bread flour, and other dry ingredients, except whole wheat flour. Combine liquids and heat to 120° to 130° F.

Hand-Held Mixer Method Combine dry mixture and liquid ingredients in mixing bowl on low speed. Beat 2 to 3 minutes on medium speed. By hand, stir in whole wheat flour and enough remaining bread flour to make a firm dough. Knead on floured surface 5 to 7 minutes or until smooth and elastic. Use additional flour if necessary.

Stand Mixer Method Combine dry mixture and liquid ingredients in mixing bowl with paddle or beaters for 4 minutes on medium speed. Gradually add whole wheat flour and remaining bread flour and knead with dough hook(s) 5 to 7 minutes until smooth and elastic.

Food Processor Method Put dry mixture in processing bowl with steel blade. While motor is running, add liquid ingredients. Process until mixed. Continue processing, adding whole wheat flour and remaining bread flour until dough forms a ball.

Rising, Shaping, and Baking

Place dough in lightly oiled bowl and turn to grease top. Cover; let rise until dough tests ripe. Turn dough onto lightly floured surface; punch down to remove air bubbles. Shape into a round loaf and place on a greased baking sheet. Cover; let rise until indentation remains after touching. With a very sharp knife, make a cross slash across the top of loaf. Bake in preheated 375° F oven 35 to 40 minutes. If the crust is getting too dark, cover loosely with foil the last 5 to 10 minutes of baking. Remove from baking sheet; cool.

Makes 1 loaf.

For years, molasses was the sweetener of choice in many parts of this country. Valued for its rich flavor and smoothness, the addition of molasses in this multi-fiber bread makes it a favorite.

Ingredients	Medium	Large
Water	1 cup + 2 tablespoons	1 ½ cups + 2 tablespoons
Vegetable oil	1 tablespoon + 1 ½ teaspoons	2 tablespoons
Molasses	3 tablespoons	4 tablespoons
Salt	1 ½ teaspoons	2 teaspoons
Wheat germ	⅓ cup	½ cup
Oatmeal	¾ cup	1 cup
Bread flour	3 cups	4 cups
Active dry yeast	2 ¼ teaspoons	1 tablespoon

Cook's Note: Due to the low volume of this loaf, the medium recipe can be used in a small machine.

Bread Machine Method

Have liquid ingredients at 80° F and all others at room temperature. Place ingredients in pan in the order specified in your owner's manual. Select basic cycle and medium/normal crust.

Mixer Methods

Using ingredient amounts listed for medium loaf, combine yeast, 1 cup flour, and other dry ingredients. Combine liquids and heat to 120° to 130° F.

Hand-Held Mixer Method Combine dry mixture and liquid ingredients in mixing bowl on low speed. Beat 2 to 3 minutes on medium speed. By hand, stir in enough remaining flour to make a firm dough. Knead on floured surface 5 to 7 minutes or until smooth and elastic. Use additional flour if necessary.

Stand Mixer Method Combine dry mixture and liquid ingredients in mixing bowl with paddle or beaters for 4 minutes on medium speed. Gradually add remaining flour and knead with dough hook(s) 5 to 7 minutes until smooth and elastic.

Food Processor Method Put dry mixture in processing bowl with steel blade. While motor is running, add liquid ingredients. Process until mixed. Continue processing, adding remaining flour until dough forms a ball.

Rising, Shaping, and Baking

Place dough in lightly oiled bowl and turn to grease top. Cover; let rise until dough tests ripe. Turn dough onto lightly floured surface; punch down to remove air bubbles. Roll or pat into a 14- x 7-inch rectangle. Starting with shorter side, roll up tightly, pressing dough into roll. Pinch edges and ends to seal. Place in greased 9- x 5-inch loaf pan. Cover; let rise until indentation remains after touching. Bake in preheated 375° F oven 30 to 40 minutes. Remove from pan; cool.

Makes 1 loaf.

Orange Walnut Bread

With the fresh, sunny flavor of orange in each bite, this special bread will brighten up even the gloomiest of mornings.

Ingredients	Medium	Large
Water	¾ cup	1 cup
Vegetable oil	2 tablespoons	3 tablespoons
Low-sugar orange marmalade	¼ cup	¼ cup + 1 tablespoon
Salt	1 ½ teaspoons	2 teaspoons
Sugar	3 tablespoons	¼ cup
Whole wheat flour	1 cup	1 ½ cups
Bread flour	2 cups	2 ½ cups
Active dry yeast	2 ¼ teaspoons	1 tablespoon
Walnuts	½ cup	⅔ cup

Cook's Note: Due to the low volume of this loaf, the medium recipe can be used in a small machine.

Bread Machine Method

Have liquid ingredients at 80° F and all others at room temperature. Place ingredients in pan in the order specified in your owner's manual. Select basic cycle and medium/normal crust. Walnuts can be added 5 minutes before the end of the last kneading cycle.

Mixer Methods

Using ingredient amounts listed for medium loaf, combine yeast, 1 cup bread flour, sugar and salt. Combine water, oil and marmalade; heat to 120° to 130° F.

Hand-Held Mixer Method Combine dry mixture and liquid ingredients in mixing bowl on low speed. Beat 2 to 3 minutes on medium speed. By hand, stir in whole wheat flour, walnuts, and enough remaining bread flour to make a firm dough. Knead on floured surface 5 to 7 minutes or until smooth and elastic. Use additional bread flour if necessary.

Stand Mixer Method Combine dry mixture and liquid ingredients in mixing bowl with paddle or beaters for 4 minutes on medium speed. Gradually add whole wheat flour, walnuts, and remaining bread flour and knead with dough hook(s) 5 to 7 minutes until smooth and elastic.

Food Processor Method Put dry mixture in processing bowl with steel blade. While motor is running, add liquid ingredients. Process until mixed. Continue processing, adding whole wheat flour and remaining bread flour until dough forms a ball. Add walnuts; pulse just until mixed.

Rising, Shaping, and Baking

Place dough in lightly oiled bowl and turn to grease top. Cover; let rise until dough tests ripe. Turn dough onto lightly floured surface; punch down to remove air bubbles. Shape into a round loaf. Place loaf on greased cookie sheet. Cover; let rise until indentation remains when touched. Combine 1 egg and 1 tablespoon water; brush top. Sprinkle with oatmeal. Bake in preheated 375° F oven 30 to 40 minutes. Remove from cookie sheet; cool.

Makes 1 loaf.

Seed and Wheat Bread

Ingredients	Medium	Large
Water	½ cup + 3 tablespoons	¾ cup + 2 tablespoons
Vegetable oil	3 tablespoons	4 tablespoons
Light molasses	4 tablespoons	5 tablespoons
Egg(s), room temperature	1	2
Flax seeds	1 tablespoon	1 tablespoon + 1 ½ teaspoons
Sesame seeds	2 tablespoons	3 tablespoons
Salt	1 ½ teaspoons	2 teaspoons
Whole wheat flour	1 cup	1 ⅓ cups
Bread flour	2 cups	2 ⅔ cups
Active dry yeast	2 ¼ teaspoons	1 tablespoon

Cook's Note: Due to the low volume of this loaf, the medium recipe can be used in a small machine.

Bread Machine Method

Have liquid ingredients at 80° F and all others at room temperature. Place ingredients in pan in the order specified in your owner's manual. Select basic cycle and medium/normal crust. Do not use the delay timer.

Mixer Methods

Using ingredient amounts listed for medium loaf, combine yeast, 1 cup bread flour, and other dry ingredients, except whole wheat flour. Combine liquids, except egg; heat to 120° to 130° F.

Hand-Held Mixer Method Combine dry mixture and liquid ingredients in mixing bowl on low speed. Beat 2 to 3 minutes on medium speed. Add egg; beat 1 minute. By hand, stir in whole wheat flour and enough remaining bread flour to make a firm dough. Knead on floured surface 5 to 7 minutes or until smooth and elastic. Use additional flour if necessary.

Stand Mixer Method Combine dry mixture and liquid ingredients in mixing bowl with paddle or beaters for 4 minutes on medium speed. Add egg; beat 1 minute. Gradually add whole wheat flour and remaining bread flour and knead with dough hook(s) 5 to 7 minutes until smooth and elastic.

Food Processor Method Put dry mixture in processing bowl with steel blade. While motor is running, add egg and liquid ingredients. Process until mixed. Continue processing, adding whole wheat flour and remaining bread flour until dough forms a ball.

Rising, Shaping, and Baking

Place dough in lightly oiled bowl and turn to grease top. Cover; let rise until dough tests ripe. Turn dough onto lightly floured surface; punch down to remove air bubbles. Roll or pat into a 14- x 7-inch rectangle. Starting with shorter side, roll up tightly, pressing dough into roll. Pinch edges and ends to seal. Place in greased 9- x 5-inch loaf pan. Cover; let rise until indentation remains after touching. Bake in preheated 375° F oven 30 to 40 minutes. Remove from pan; cool.

Makes 1 loaf.

Whole Wheat Honey Bread

Out of all the recipes in our collection, Whole Wheat Honey Bread, best known as Honey of a Whole Wheat Bread, is our most requested recipe.

Ingredients	Small	Medium	Large
Water	—	3 tablespoons	1 tablespoon
Milk	⅓ cup	½ cup	⅔ cup
Egg, room temperature	1	1	1
Vegetable oil	1 tablespoon	2 tablespoons	3 tablespoons
Honey	2 tablespoons	¼ cup	¼ cup + 2 tablespoons
Salt	1 teaspoon	1 ½ teaspoons	2 teaspoons
Whole wheat flour	⅔ cup	1 cup	1 ⅓ cups
Bread flour	1 ⅓ cups	2 cups	2 ⅔ cups
Active dry yeast	1 ½ teaspoons	2 ¼ teaspoons	1 tablespoon

Bread Machine Method

Have liquid ingredients at 80° F and all others at room temperature. Place ingredients in pan in the order specified in your owner's manual. Select basic cycle and medium/normal crust. Do not use the delay timer.

Mixer Methods

Using ingredient amounts listed for medium loaf, combine yeast, 1 cup bread flour, and salt. Combine liquids, except egg, and heat to 120° to 130° F.

Hand-Held Mixer Method Combine dry mixture and liquid ingredients in mixing bowl on low speed. Beat 2 to 3 minutes on medium speed. Add egg; beat 1 minute. By hand, stir in whole wheat flour and enough remaining bread flour to make a firm dough. Knead on floured surface 5 to 7 minutes or until smooth and elastic. Use additional bread flour if necessary.

Stand Mixer Method Combine dry mixture and liquid ingredients in mixing bowl with paddle or beaters for 4 minutes on medium speed. Add egg; beat 1 minute. Gradually add whole wheat flour and remaining bread flour and knead with dough hook(s) 5 to 7 minutes until smooth and elastic.

Food Processor Method Put dry mixture in processing bowl with steel blade. While motor is running, add egg and liquid ingredients. Process until mixed. Continue processing, adding whole wheat flour and remaining bread flour until dough forms a ball.

Rising, Shaping, and Baking

Place dough in lightly oiled bowl and turn to grease top. Cover; let rise until dough tests ripe. Turn dough onto lightly floured surface; punch down to remove air bubbles. Roll or pat into a 14- x 7-inch rectangle. Starting with shorter side, roll up tightly, pressing dough into roll. Pinch edges and ends to seal. Place in greased 9- x 5-inch loaf pan. Cover; let rise until indentation remains after touching. Bake in preheated 375° F oven 30 to 40 minutes. Remove from pan; cool.

Makes 1 loaf.

Oatmeal Breakfast Bread

From our RED STAR® Yeast & Products Baker's Collection, Oatmeal Breakfast Bread is a family favorite from Sandra Pulido of Austin, Texas. We are certain that it will become a favorite at your house, too.

Ingredients	Medium	Large
Water	1 cup + 2 tablespoons	1 ¼ cups + 1 tablespoon
Vegetable oil	1 tablespoon	1 tablespoon + 2 teaspoons
Maple syrup	⅓ cup	½ cup
Ground cinnamon	2 teaspoons	2 ½ teaspoons
Salt	1 teaspoon	1 ¼ teaspoons
Oatmeal	1 cup	1 ¼ cups
Bread flour	3 cups	4 cups
Active dry yeast	2 ¼ teaspoons	1 tablespoon
Pecans	1 cup	1 ¼ cups
Raisins	1 cup	1 ¼ cups

Cook's Note: Due to the low volume of this loaf, the medium recipe can be used in a small machine.

Bread Machine Method

Have liquid ingredients at 80° F and all others at room temperature. Place ingredients in pan in the order specified in your owner's manual. Select basic cycle and medium/normal crust. Pecans and raisins can be added 5 minutes before the end of the last kneading cycle.

Mixer Methods

Using ingredient amounts listed for medium loaf, combine yeast, 1 cup flour, and other dry ingredients, except pecans and raisins. Combine liquids and heat to 120° to 130° F.

Hand-Held Mixer Method Combine dry mixture and liquid ingredients in mixing bowl on low speed. Beat 2 to 3 minutes on medium speed. By hand, stir in pecans, raisins, and enough remaining flour to make a firm dough. Knead on floured surface 5 to 7 minutes or until smooth and elastic. Use additional flour if necessary.

Stand Mixer Method Combine dry mixture and liquid ingredients in mixing bowl with paddle or beaters for 4 minutes on medium speed. Gradually add pecans, raisins, and remaining flour and knead with dough hook(s) 5 to 7 minutes until smooth and elastic.

Food Processor Method Put dry mixture in processing bowl with steel blade. While motor is running, add liquid ingredients. Process until mixed. Continue processing, adding remaining flour until dough forms a ball. Add pecans and raisins; pulse just until mixed.

Rising, Shaping, and Baking

Place dough in lightly oiled bowl and turn to grease top. Cover; let rise until dough tests ripe. Turn dough onto lightly floured surface; punch down to remove air bubbles. Roll or pat into a 14- x 7-inch rectangle. Starting with shorter side, roll up tightly, pressing dough into roll. Pinch edges and ends to seal. Place in greased 9- x 5-inch loaf pan. Cover; let rise until indentation remains after touching. Bake in preheated 375° F oven 30 to 40 minutes. Remove from pan; cool.

Makes 1 loaf.

Chapter 4
Loaves From Starters

Sourdough, a mainstay of meals for pioneers, trappers, prospectors, and early settlers, is a part of our country's cultural heritage. As recently as the early 1900s, the only bread that was served with the family dinner was one that had been started days before. A large bowl containing flour, water, and a little sugar was set on a shelf in hopes of gathering "wild" yeast. After several days, the mixture would begin to bubble and grow, letting everyone know that bread would be following shortly. This crusty bread with a slightly sour taste was a special treat and looked forward to by the entire family.

Sourdough bread is a gourmet delight! Today, one who has a discriminating taste for fine bread will be delighted to find the recipes included in this chapter. They are hearty, chewy and moist breads—very satisfying to the palate and the appetite.

The anticipation of the flavor begins when the pungent yeasty aroma from the starter fills the air. Anyone entering the kitchen will know something unique is in preparation—and right they are, for the starter will give the sourdough its individuality. No two starters are exactly the same, as the activity of the yeast varies depending on the flour, the room temperature, the humidity, and the aura of the baker. Therefore, each sourdough will have its own character.

This chapter provides a variety from which to choose. Sourdough Pancakes are so delicious, you will be hard pressed to match them with any others. Beginning a whole wheat bread with a whole wheat starter adds a tangy zest to the nutty flavor of wheat. The texture will be so fine you will think the bread was made from cake flour. Old Milwaukee Rye Bread uses the wonderful quality of rye flour to ferment easily; thus, a savory rye bread is created.

Making sourdough requires planning ahead but not a lot of your time. (The yeast is doing the work!) It is definitely worth the effort on your part.

Sourdough Starter

Making a starter at home today is relatively easy when using active dry yeast. Plan to prepare your starter a few days before you wish to bake so that it has ample time to develop. As you will see, starters can be made with white, whole wheat, and even rye flour, each imparting its own distinct characteristics to the finished bread.

Ingredients

Active dry yeast	2 ¼ teaspoons	**Bread flour**	3 ½ cups
Water	2 cups	**Sugar**	1 tablespoon

In a 4-quart nonmetallic container, dissolve yeast in warm water (110° to 115° F); let stand 5 minutes. Add flour and sugar. Stir by hand until blended. The mixture will be thick; any remaining lumps will dissolve during the fermentation process. Cover loosely with plastic wrap. Let stand in warm place for 5 days, stirring 2 to 3 times each day. The starter will rise and fall during the fermentation period; it becomes thinner as it stands. A temperature of 80° to 85° F is best for developing the sour flavor. When the starter is developed, it is bubbly and may have a yellow liquid layer on top; stir starter before using. The starter can be used for baking or placed in the refrigerator for later use.

To use the starter, measure out desired amount as specified in the recipe. Let refrigerated starter come to room temperature before using; this will take about 4 hours.

Replenish remaining starter with 3 parts flour to 2 parts water and 1 teaspoon sugar. Stir until blended; some lumps may remain. Cover loosely and let stand in warm place for 10 to 12 hours or overnight. The starter will rise and become bubbly. Stir and store in refrigerator.

If the starter is not used every week, stir in 1 teaspoon sugar to keep it active.

Sourdough Pancakes

Before the days of baking powder, pancakes were made with a wild yeast starter. These simple to make pancakes are sure to become a breakfast favorite.

Ingredients

All-purpose flour	1 ¼ cups	**Vegetable oil**	1 tablespoon
Milk	1 cup	**Baking soda**	1 teaspoon
Sourdough starter (see above)	½ cup	**Sugar**	1 tablespoon
Salt	½ teaspoon	**Egg,** room temperature	1

In large mixing bowl, combine flour, milk, and starter. Let stand for 30 minutes. By hand, stir in remaining ingredients (batter will be slightly lumpy). Pour about ¼ cup batter onto lightly greased, preheated 450° F electric griddle or fry pan. Cook until bottoms are golden brown and bubbles are breaking on the surface. Turn and cook other side.

Makes about 12 4-inch pancakes or 44 silver-dollar-size pancakes.

Scandinavian Rye Bread

Scandinavians have been using rye flour for generations in making their characteristic flat breads and hearty rye loaves. The following recipe makes a wonderfully chewy loaf of bread.

Ingredients	Small	Medium	Large
Water	½ cup + 1 tablespoon	¾ cup	1 cup
Vegetable oil	1 tablespoon	2 tablespoons	3 tablespoons
Sourdough starter (page 58)	¾ cup	1 cup	1 ¼ cups
Salt	1 teaspoon	1 ½ teaspoons	2 teaspoons
Sugar	2 teaspoons	1 tablespoon	1 tablespoon + 1 teaspoon
Caraway seeds	1 ½ teaspoons	2 teaspoons	2 ½ teaspoons
Rye flour	½ cup	1 cup	1 ½ cups
Bread flour	2 cups	2 cups	2 ½ cups
Active dry yeast	1 ½ teaspoons	2 ¼ teaspoons	1 tablespoon

Bread Machine Method

Have water and oil at 80° F and all other ingredients at room temperature. Place ingredients in pan in the order specified in your owner's manual. Select basic cycle and medium/normal crust. Do not use the delay timer.

Mixer Methods

Using ingredient amounts listed for medium loaf, combine yeast, 1 cup bread flour, and other dry ingredients, except rye flour. Combine water and oil; heat to 120° to 130° F.

Hand-Held Mixer Method Combine sourdough starter, dry mixture, and liquid ingredients in mixing bowl on low speed. Beat 2 to 3 minutes on medium speed. By hand, stir in rye flour and enough remaining bread flour to make a firm dough. Knead on floured surface 5 to 7 minutes or until smooth and elastic. Use additional bread flour if necessary.

Stand Mixer Method Combine sourdough starter, dry mixture, and liquid ingredients in mixing bowl with paddle or beaters for 4 minutes on medium speed. Gradually add rye flour and remaining bread flour and knead with dough hook(s) 5 to 7 minutes until smooth and elastic.

Food Processor Method Put sourdough starter and dry mixture in processing bowl with steel blade. While motor is running, add liquid ingredients. Process until mixed. Continue processing, adding rye flour and remaining bread flour until dough forms a ball.

Rising, Shaping, and Baking

Place dough in lightly oiled bowl and turn to grease top. Cover; let rise until dough tests ripe. Turn dough onto lightly floured surface; punch down to remove air bubbles. Shape into a round loaf. Place on greased cookie sheet. Cover; let rise until indentation remains after touching. With a very sharp knife, make an "X" on the top of loaf. Bake in preheated 375° F oven 30 to 40 minutes. Remove from pan; cool.

Makes 1 loaf.

Sourdough Cracked Wheat Rolls

Simple to make, these sourdough rolls have the added flavor and texture of cracked wheat.

Ingredients

Water	¾ cup
Vegetable oil	1 tablespoon
Sourdough starter (page 58)	1 cup
Salt	2 teaspoons
Sugar	1 tablespoon
Cracked wheat	⅓ cup
Bread flour	3 cups
Active dry yeast	2 ¼ teaspoons

Bread Machine Method

Have water and oil at 80° F and all other ingredients at room temperature. Place ingredients in pan in the order specified in your owner's manual. Select dough/manual cycle. Do not use the delay timer.

Mixer Methods

Combine yeast, 1 cup flour, and other dry ingredients. Combine water and oil; heat to 120° to 130° F.

Hand-Held Mixer Method Combine sourdough starter, dry mixture, and liquid ingredients in mixing bowl on low speed. Beat 2 to 3 minutes on medium speed. By hand, stir in enough remaining flour to make a firm dough. Knead on floured surface 5 to 7 minutes or until smooth and elastic. Use additional flour if necessary. Place dough in lightly oiled bowl and turn to grease top. Cover; let rise until dough tests ripe.

Stand Mixer Method Combine sourdough starter, dry mixture, and liquid ingredients in mixing bowl with paddle or beaters for 4 minutes on medium speed. Gradually add remaining flour and knead with dough hook(s) 5 to 7 minutes until smooth and elastic. Place dough in lightly oiled bowl and turn to grease top. Cover; let rise until dough tests ripe.

Food Processor Method Put sourdough starter and dry mixture in processing bowl with steel blade. While motor is running, add liquid ingredients. Process until mixed. Continue processing, adding remaining flour until dough forms a ball. Place dough in lightly oiled bowl and turn to grease top. Cover; let rise until dough tests ripe.

Shaping and Baking

Turn dough onto lightly floured surface; punch down to remove air bubbles. Divide dough into 8 pieces. On lightly floured surface, roll each piece to a 6- x 4-inch rectangle. Starting with the longer side, roll up tightly, pressing dough into roll with each turn. Pinch edges and ends to seal. Place on greased cookie sheet. Cover; let rise until doubled. With sharp knife, make a lengthwise slash down the center of each roll. Brush with cold water. Bake in preheated 400° F oven 20 to 25 minutes or until brown. Remove from cookie sheet; cool.

Makes 8 rolls.

San Francisco Sourdough Bread

With a crisp crust, a light crumb, and a tangy taste, the following recipe is an excellent version of the world-famous bread from the City by the Bay.

Ingredients	Small	Medium	Large
Water	½ cup + 1 tablespoon	¾ cup + 1 tablespoon	¾ cup + 2 tablespoons
Sourdough starter (page 58)	¾ cup	1 cup	1 ¼ cups
Salt	1 ½ teaspoons	2 teaspoons	2 ½ teaspoons
Sugar	2 teaspoons	1 tablespoon	1 tablespoon + 1 teaspoon
Bread flour	2 ¼ cups	3 cups	4 cups
Active dry yeast	1 ½ teaspoons	2 ¼ teaspoons	1 tablespoon

Bread Machine Method

Have water at 80° F and all other ingredients at room temperature. Place ingredients in pan in the order specified in your owner's manual. Select basic cycle and medium/normal crust. Do not use the delay timer.

Mixer Methods

Using ingredient amounts listed for medium loaf, combine yeast, 1 cup flour, and other dry ingredients. Heat water to 120° to 130° F.

Hand-Held Mixer Method Combine sourdough starter, dry mixture, and water in mixing bowl on low speed. Beat 2 to 3 minutes on medium speed. By hand, stir in enough remaining flour to make a firm dough. Knead on floured surface 5 to 7 minutes or until smooth and elastic. Use additional flour if necessary.

Stand Mixer Method Combine sourdough starter, dry mixture, and water in mixing bowl with paddle or beaters for 4 minutes on medium speed. Gradually add remaining flour and knead with dough hook(s) 5 to 7 minutes until smooth and elastic.

Food Processor Method Put sourdough starter and dry mixture in processing bowl with steel blade. While motor is running, add water. Process until mixed. Continue processing, adding remaining flour until dough forms a ball.

Rising, Shaping, and Baking

Place dough in lightly oiled bowl and turn to grease top. Cover; let rise until dough tests ripe. Turn dough onto lightly floured surface; punch down to remove air bubbles. Roll or pat into a 12- x 5-inch rectangle. Starting with shorter side, roll up tightly, pressing dough into roll. Pinch edges and taper ends to seal. Place on greased cookie sheet sprinkled with cornmeal. Cover; let rise until indentation remains after touching. With very sharp knife, make 2 or 3 diagonal slashes across top of loaf. Spray or brush loaf with cold water. Bake in preheated 400° F oven 30 to 35 minutes. For a crisper crust, spray or brush loaf with cold water several times during the first 12 minutes of baking. Remove from cookie sheet; cool.

Makes 1 baguette.

Sourdough Sandwich Rolls

These rolls are an excellent choice for burgers and sandwiches.

Ingredients

Water	¾ cup
Sourdough starter (page 58)	1 cup
Vegetable oil	1 tablespoon
Egg, room temperature	1
Salt	1 ½ teaspoons
Sugar	1 tablespoon
Bread flour	3 cups
Active dry yeast	2 ¼ teaspoons

Bread Machine Method

Have water and oil at 80° F and all other ingredients at room temperature. Place ingredients in pan in the order specified in your owner's manual. Select dough/manual cycle. Do not use the delay timer.

Mixer Methods

Combine yeast, 1 cup flour, salt and sugar. Combine water and oil; heat to 120° to 130° F.

Hand-Held Mixer Method Combine sourdough starter, dry mixture, and liquid ingredients in mixing bowl on low speed. Beat 2 to 3 minutes on medium speed. Add egg and beat 1 minute. By hand, stir in enough remaining flour to make a firm dough. Knead on floured surface 5 to 7 minutes or until smooth and elastic. Use additional flour if necessary. Place dough in lightly oiled bowl and turn to grease top. Cover; let rise until dough tests ripe.

Stand Mixer Method Combine sourdough starter, dry mixture, and liquid ingredients in mixing bowl with paddle or beaters for 4 minutes on medium speed. Add egg and beat 1 minute. Gradually add remaining flour and knead with dough hook(s) 5 to 7 minutes until smooth and elastic. Place dough in lightly oiled bowl and turn to grease top. Cover; let rise until dough tests ripe.

Food Processor Method Put sourdough starter and dry mixture in processing bowl with steel blade. While motor is running, add egg and liquid ingredients. Process until mixed. Continue processing, adding remaining flour until dough forms a ball. Place dough in lightly oiled bowl and turn to grease top. Cover; let rise until dough tests ripe.

Shaping and Baking

Turn dough onto lightly floured surface; punch down to remove air bubbles. Divide dough into 8 pieces. On lightly floured surface, shape each piece into a smooth ball. Place on greased cookie sheet. Flatten to a 4-inch diameter. Cover; let rise until indentation remains after touching. With sharp knife, make an "X" on the top of each roll. Combine 1 egg and 1 tablespoon water. Brush tops of rolls. Bake in preheated 400° F oven 15 to 20 minutes. Remove from cookie sheet; cool.

Makes 8 rolls.

Sourdough English Muffins

Full of nooks and crannies, these wonderful English muffins will turn any morning into a special day.

Ingredients

Water	½ cup
Vegetable oil	2 tablespoons
Sourdough starter (page 58)	1 cup
Salt	1 teaspoon
Sugar	1 tablespoon
Bread flour	3 cups
Active dry yeast	2 ¼ teaspoons

Bread Machine Method

Have water and oil at 80° F and all other ingredients at room temperature. Place ingredients in pan in the order specified in your owner's manual. Select dough/manual cycle. Do not use the delay timer.

Mixer Methods

Combine yeast, 1 cup flour, salt and sugar. Combine water and oil; heat to 120° to 130° F.

Hand-Held Mixer Method Combine sourdough starter, dry mixture, and liquid ingredients in mixing bowl on low speed. Beat 2 to 3 minutes on medium speed. By hand, stir in enough remaining flour to make a firm dough. Knead on floured surface 5 to 7 minutes or until smooth and elastic. Use additional flour if necessary. Place dough in lightly oiled bowl and turn to grease top. Cover; let rise until dough tests ripe.

Stand Mixer Method Combine sourdough starter, dry mixture, and liquid ingredients in mixing bowl with paddle or beaters for 4 minutes on medium speed. Gradually add remaining flour and knead with dough hook(s) 5 to 7 minutes until smooth and elastic. Place dough in lightly oiled bowl and turn to grease top. Cover; let rise until dough tests ripe.

Food Processor Method Put sourdough starter and dry mixture in processing bowl with steel blade. While motor is running, add liquid ingredients. Process until mixed. Continue processing, adding remaining flour until dough forms a ball. Place dough in lightly oiled bowl and turn to grease top. Cover; let rise until dough tests ripe.

Shaping and Baking

On surface sprinkled with cornmeal, roll dough to ¼-inch thickness. Cut into 14 to 16 circles (3 to 4 inches in diameter). Turn to coat top side with cornmeal. Place on greased cookie sheet. Cover; let rise until doubled. Carefully place muffins on a greased and preheated 325° F electric griddle or fry pan. Bake 10 minutes on each side or until sides are deep golden brown. Cool. To serve, split and toast.

Makes 14 to 16 muffins.

Whole Wheat Sourdough Starter

Ingredients

Active dry yeast	2 ¼ teaspoons
Water	2 cups
Whole wheat flour	3 ½ cups
Sugar	1 tablespoon

In a 4-quart nonmetallic container, dissolve yeast in warm water (110° to 115° F); let stand 5 minutes. Add whole wheat flour and sugar. Stir until blended. The mixture will be thick; any remaining lumps will dissolve during the fermentation process. Cover loosely with plastic wrap. Let stand in warm place for 5 days, stirring 2 to 3 times each day. The starter will rise and fall during the fermentation period; it becomes thinner as it stands. A temperature of 80° to 85° F is best for developing the sour flavor. When the starter is developed, it is bubbly and may have a yellow liquid layer on top; stir starter before using. The starter can be used for baking or placed in the refrigerator for later use.

To use the starter, measure out desired amount as specified in the recipe. Let refrigerated starter come to room temperature before using; this will take about 4 hours.

Replenish remaining starter with 3 parts whole wheat flour to 2 parts water and 1 teaspoon sugar. Stir until blended; some lumps may remain. Cover loosely and let stand in warm place for 10 to 12 hours or overnight. The starter will rise and become bubbly. Stir and store in refrigerator.

If the starter is not used every week, stir in 1 teaspoon sugar to keep it active.

Whole Wheat Sourdough Bread

With the added goodness of the whole wheat starter and flour, this dough can be used either to make loaves or to shape into sandwich or dinner rolls.

Ingredients	Small	Medium	Large
Water	½ cup + 3 tablespoons	¾ cup + 2 tablespoons	1 cup + 3 tablespoons
Vegetable oil	1 tablespoon + 1 teaspoon	2 tablespoons	2 tablespoons + 2 teaspoons
Whole wheat sourdough starter (page 64)	¾ cup	1 cup	1 ¼ cups
Salt	1 teaspoon	1 ½ teaspoons	2 teaspoons
Sugar	2 teaspoons	1 tablespoon	1 tablespoon + 1 teaspoon
Whole wheat flour	2 ¼ cups	3 cups	4 cups
Active dry yeast	1 ½ teaspoons	2 ¼ teaspoons	1 tablespoon

Bread Machine Method

Have water and oil at 80° F and all other ingredients at room temperature. Place ingredients in pan in the order specified in your owner's manual. Select whole wheat or basic cycle and medium/normal crust. Do not use the delay timer.

Mixer Methods

Using ingredient amounts listed for medium loaf, combine yeast, 1 cup flour, and other dry ingredients. Combine water and oil; heat to 120° to 130° F.

Hand-Held Mixer Method Combine sourdough starter, dry mixture, and liquid ingredients in mixing bowl on low speed. Beat 2 to 3 minutes on medium speed. By hand, stir in enough remaining flour to make a firm dough. Knead on floured surface 5 to 7 minutes or until smooth and elastic. Use additional flour if necessary.

Stand Mixer Method Combine sourdough starter, dry mixture, and liquid ingredients in mixing bowl with paddle or beaters for 4 minutes on medium speed. Gradually add remaining flour and knead with dough hook(s) 5 to 7 minutes until smooth and elastic.

Food Processor Method Put sourdough starter and dry mixture in processing bowl with steel blade. While motor is running, add liquid ingredients. Process until mixed. Continue processing, adding remaining flour until dough forms a ball.

Rising, Shaping, and Baking

Place dough in lightly oiled bowl and turn to grease top. Cover; let rise until dough tests ripe. Turn dough onto lightly floured surface; punch down to remove air bubbles. Roll or pat into a 14- x 7-inch rectangle. Starting with shorter side, roll up tightly, pressing dough into roll. Pinch edges and ends to seal. Place in greased 9- x 5-inch loaf pan. Cover; let rise until indentation remains after touching. Bake in preheated 375° F oven 30 to 40 minutes. Remove from pan; cool.

Makes 1 loaf.

Rye Sourdough Starter

Ingredients

Active dry yeast	2 ¼ teaspoons
Water	1 ½ cups
Rye flour	2 cups
Caraway seeds	1 tablespoon

In a 4-quart nonmetallic container, dissolve yeast in warm water (110° to 115° F); let stand 5 minutes. Add rye flour and caraway seeds; stir. Cover loosely with plastic wrap; let stand in warm place 2 to 3 days. Stir twice each day. The starter will rise and fall during the fermentation period. It will become thinner as it stands. A temperature of 80° to 85° F is best for developing the sour flavor. When the starter is developed, it is bubbly and may have a yellow liquid layer on top; stir starter before using. The starter can be used for baking or placed in the refrigerator for later use.

To use the starter, measure out the desired amount as specified in the recipe. Let refrigerated starter come to room temperature before using; this will take about 4 hours.

Replenish remaining starter with 3 parts rye flour to 2 parts water and 1 teaspoon sugar. Stir until blended; some lumps may remain. Cover loosely and let stand in warm place for 10 to 12 hours or overnight. The starter will rise and become bubbly. Stir and store in refrigerator.

If the starter is not used every week, stir in 1 teaspoon sugar to keep it active.

Old Milwaukee Rye Bread

It is no surprise that Milwaukee is a "city of rye." In this city settled and inhabited by people of German, Scandinavian, and Eastern European descent, rye is the bread of choice.

Ingredients	Small	Medium	Large
Water	½ cup	¾ cup	¾ cup
Vegetable oil	1 tablespoon	4 teaspoons	5 teaspoons
Molasses	2 teaspoons	3 teaspoons	4 teaspoons
Rye sourdough starter (page 66)	½ cup	¾ cup	1 cup
Caraway seeds	1 teaspoon	1 ½ teaspoons	2 teaspoons
Salt	1 ½ teaspoons	2 teaspoons	2 ½ teaspoons
Rye flour	⅓ cup	½ cup	⅔ cup
Bread flour	1 ½ cups	2 cups	2 ⅔ cups
Active dry yeast	1 ½ teaspoons	2 ¼ teaspoons	1 tablespoon

Bread Machine Method

Have water, oil, and molasses at 80° F and all other ingredients at room temperature. Place ingredients in pan in the order specified in your owner's manual. Select basic cycle and medium/normal crust. Do not use the delay timer.

Mixer Methods

Using ingredient amounts listed for medium loaf, combine yeast, 1 cup bread flour, caraway seeds, and salt. Combine water, oil, and molasses; heat to 120° to 130° F.

Hand-Held Mixer Method Combine sourdough starter, dry mixture, and liquid ingredients in mixing bowl on low speed. Beat 2 to 3 minutes on medium speed. By hand, stir in rye flour and enough remaining bread flour to make a firm dough. Knead on floured surface 5 to 7 minutes or until smooth and elastic. Use additional bread flour if necessary.

Stand Mixer Method Combine sourdough starter, dry mixture, and liquid ingredients in mixing bowl with paddle or beaters for 4 minutes on medium speed. Gradually add rye flour and remaining bread flour and knead with dough hook(s) 5 to 7 minutes until smooth and elastic.

Food Processor Method Put sourdough starter and dry mixture in processing bowl with steel blade. While motor is running, add liquid ingredients. Process until mixed. Continue processing, adding rye flour and remaining bread flour until dough forms a ball.

Rising, Shaping, and Baking

Place dough in lightly oiled bowl and turn to grease top. Cover; let rise until dough tests ripe. Turn dough onto lightly floured surface; punch down to remove air bubbles. Shape dough into a round loaf. Place on greased cookie sheet sprinkled with cornmeal. Cover; let rise 15 minutes. With sharp knife, make 2 or 3 slashes on the top of the loaf. Let rise again until indentation remains after touching. Bake in preheated 375° F oven 40 to 45 minutes. Remove from cookie sheet; cool.

Makes 1 round loaf.

Chapter 5
Rolls, Flat Breads, and Braided Loaves

One of the many pleasures of bread making is shaping the dough with your hands. Everyone loves the feel of yeast dough. It's a wonderful opportunity to share the fun of bread making with others. Children of all ages will be grateful to work with dough. You will be pleasantly surprised to see how simple it is to make these breads using the easy-to-follow recipes and the directions for shaping.

While you are working together you may want to recall the origin of the recipe. Rolls, Flat Breads, and Braided Loaves presents a cross-cultural representation of yeast breads brought over by our immigrant forefathers: French croissants, Jewish bagels, Italian pizza, German pretzels—all have crossed cultural boundaries. Today, they are truly American.

New York Bagels

If you have ever experienced a real New York bagel, you will know that the bagels sold in the frozen food section of most supermarkets pale in taste and texture. Boiling the bagels in water before baking them is what gives them their distinctive, chewy texture.

Ingredients

Water	1 cup
Salt	1 teaspoon
Sugar	2 tablespoons
Bread flour	3 cups
Active dry yeast	2 ¼ teaspoons

Bread Machine Method

Have water at 80° F and all other ingredients at room temperature. Place ingredients in pan in the order specified in your owner's manual. Select dough/manual cycle. Do not use the delay timer.

Mixer Methods

Combine yeast, 1 cup flour, salt, and sugar. Heat water to 120° to 130° F.

Hand-Held Mixer Method Combine dry mixture and water in mixing bowl on low speed. Beat 2 to 3 minutes on medium speed. By hand, stir in enough remaining flour to make a firm dough. Knead on floured surface 5 to 7 minutes or until smooth and elastic. Use additional flour if necessary. Place dough in lightly oiled bowl and turn to grease top. Cover; let rise until dough tests ripe.

Stand Mixer Method Combine dry mixture and water in mixing bowl with paddle or beaters for 4 minutes on medium speed. Gradually add remaining flour and knead with dough hook(s) 5 to 7 minutes until smooth and elastic. Place dough in lightly oiled bowl and turn to grease top. Cover; let rise until dough tests ripe.

Food Processor Method Put dry mixture in processing bowl with steel blade. While motor is running, add water. Process until mixed. Continue processing, adding remaining flour until dough forms a ball. Place in lightly oiled bowl and turn to grease top. Cover; let rise until dough tests ripe.

Shaping and Baking

Turn dough onto lightly floured surface; punch down to remove air bubbles. Divide dough into 4 parts and each part into 3 pieces. On lightly floured surface, shape each piece into a smooth ball. Punch a hole in the center with a finger. Pull dough gently to make a 1 to 2-inch hole. Heat 2 quarts water and 2 tablespoons sugar to boiling. Place a few bagels at a time in boiling water. Simmer 3 minutes, turning once. Remove with a slotted spoon. Place on greased cookie sheets. Brush tops with 1 slightly beaten egg white; sprinkle with poppy or sesame seeds. Bake in preheated 375° F oven 20 to 25 minutes or until golden brown. Remove from cookie sheets; cool.

Makes 12 bagels.

Cook's Note: If an egg bagel is preferred, reduce water to ¾ cup and add 1 egg at room temperature.

Pizza Dough and Variations

After hamburgers, pizza is the second favorite fast food in the United States.

Ingredients

Water	1 cup
Olive oil	2 tablespoons
Salt	1 teaspoon
Bread flour	3 cups
Active dry yeast	2 ¼ teaspoons

Bread Machine Method

Have liquid ingredients at 80° F, all others at room temperature. Place ingredients in pan in the order specified in your owner's manual. Select dough/manual cycle. At the end of the last kneading cycle, press STOP/CLEAR, remove dough and proceed with rising, shaping, and baking instructions.

Mixer Methods

Combine yeast, 1 cup flour, and salt. Combine liquids and heat to 120° to 130° F.

Hand-Held Mixer Method Combine dry mixture and liquid ingredients in mixing bowl on low speed. Beat 2 to 3 minutes on medium speed. By hand, stir in enough remaining flour to make a firm dough. Knead on floured surface 5 to 7 minutes or until smooth and elastic. Use additional flour if necessary.

Stand Mixer Method Combine dry mixture and liquid ingredients in mixing bowl with paddle or beaters for 4 minutes on medium speed. Gradually add remaining flour and knead with dough hook(s) 5 to 7 minutes until smooth and elastic.

Food Processor Method Put dry mixture in processing bowl with steel blade. While motor is running, add liquid ingredients. Process until mixed. Continue processing, adding remaining flour until dough forms a ball.

Rising, Shaping, and Baking

Let dough rest 15 minutes. Divide into 2 parts. Press each half into a generously greased 12-inch round pizza pan sprinkled with cornmeal. Prebake for 10 to 12 minutes in preheated 400° F oven until edges of crust begin to turn light golden brown. Add desired toppings and bake an additional 15 minutes.

Makes two 12-inch crusts.

Cook's Note: A whole wheat crust can be made by substituting 1 cup whole wheat flour and 2 cups bread flour for the 3 cups of bread flour called for in the recipe. A cheese crust can be made by adding ¼ cup grated Parmesan cheese and 1 teaspoon Italian seasoning blend to the original recipe.

Pizza Sauce and Toppings

Ingredients

Oregano	¼ teaspoon
Basil	¼ teaspoon
Black pepper	¼ teaspoon
Garlic powder	⅛ teaspoon
Onion powder	⅛ teaspoon
Parmesan cheese	2 teaspoons
Salt	½ teaspoon
Tomato puree	10 ¾ ounces

Mix all ingredients together. Makes enough sauce for two 12-inch pizzas.

Cook's Note: One teaspoon Italian seasoning and ½ teaspoon dried minced onion can be substituted for the oregano, basil, pepper, garlic powder, and onion powder.

Suggested Pizza Toppings: Sliced ripe or green olives, chopped green peppers, sliced mushrooms, chopped onions, variety of cheeses, Italian sausage, sliced pepperoni, ground turkey, chicken, or beef, cooked shellfish, or a variety of vegetables can be used in any combination.

Focaccia

Over the past few years, it seems like everyone has been talking about focaccia, a wonderful, chewy Italian flatbread. Unlike pizza, focaccia is usually just brushed with rich olive oil and, perhaps, sprinkled with coarse salt and coarsely chopped herbs like sage, basil, and oregano.

Ingredients

Water	1 cup
Olive oil	1 tablespoon
Salt	1 teaspoon
Sugar	1 tablespoon
Bread flour	3 cups
Active dry yeast	2 ¼ teaspoons

Bread Machine Method

Have liquid ingredients at 80° F and all others at room temperature. Place ingredients in pan in the order specified in your owner's manual. Select dough/manual cycle. Do not use the delay timer.

Mixer Methods

Combine yeast, 1 cup flour, salt, and sugar. Combine water and oil; heat to 120° to 130° F.

Hand-Held Mixer Method Combine dry mixture and liquid ingredients in mixing bowl on low speed. Beat 2 to 3 minutes on medium speed. By hand, stir in enough remaining flour to make a firm dough. Knead on floured surface 5 to 7 minutes or until smooth and elastic. Use additional flour if necessary. Place dough in lightly oiled bowl and turn to grease top. Cover; let rise until dough tests ripe.

Stand Mixer Method Combine dry mixture and liquid ingredients in mixing bowl with paddle or beaters for 4 minutes on medium speed. Gradually add remaining flour and knead with dough hook(s) 5 to 7 minutes until smooth and elastic. Place dough in lightly oiled bowl and turn to grease top. Cover; let rise until dough tests ripe.

Food Processor Method Put dry mixture in processing bowl with steel blade. While motor is running, add liquid ingredients. Process until mixed. Continue processing, adding remaining flour until dough forms a ball. Place dough in lightly oiled bowl and turn to grease top. Cover; let rise until dough tests ripe.

Shaping and Baking

Turn dough onto lightly floured surface; punch down to remove air bubbles. On lightly floured surface, shape dough into a ball. Place on greased cookie sheet. Flatten to a 14-inch circle. With a table knife, cut a circle in dough about 1 inch from edge, cutting almost through to the cookie sheet. Prick center with a fork. Cover; let rise about 15 minutes. Brush with olive oil and sprinkle with desired toppings. Bake in preheated 375° F oven 25 to 30 minutes or until golden brown. Remove from cookie sheet to cool. Serve warm or cold.

Makes one 14-inch crust.

Suggested Focaccia Toppings: sun-dried tomatoes, grilled green pepper slices, sautéed onion rings, fresh and dried herbs of any combination, and grated hard cheese.

Calzone

Like a pocket pizza, calzone, which means "stuffed pants" in Italian, can be a meal in itself.

Ingredients

Water	1 cup
Olive oil	2 tablespoons
Salt	1 ½ teaspoons
Bread flour	2 ½ cups
Active dry yeast	2 ¼ teaspoons

Bread Machine Method

Have liquid ingredients at 80° F and all others at room temperature. Place ingredients in pan in the order specified in your owner's manual. Select dough/manual cycle. Do not use the delay timer.

Mixer Methods

Combine yeast, 1 cup flour, and salt. Combine liquids and heat to 120° to 130° F.

Hand-Held Mixer Method Combine dry mixture and liquid ingredients in mixing bowl on low speed. Beat 2 to 3 minutes on medium speed. By hand, stir in enough remaining flour to make a firm dough. Knead on floured surface 5 to 7 minutes or until smooth and elastic. Use additional flour if necessary. Place dough in lightly oiled bowl and turn to grease top. Cover; let rise until dough tests ripe.

Stand Mixer Method Combine dry mixture and liquid ingredients in mixing bowl with paddle or beaters for 4 minutes on medium speed. Gradually add remaining flour and knead with dough hook(s) 5 to 7 minutes until smooth and elastic. Place dough in lightly oiled bowl and turn to grease top. Cover; let rise until dough tests ripe.

Food Processor Method Put dry mixture in processing bowl with steel blade. While motor is running, add liquid ingredients. Process until mixed. Continue processing, adding remaining flour until dough forms a ball. Place in lightly oiled bowl and turn to grease top. Cover; let rise until dough tests ripe.

Shaping and Baking

Turn dough onto lightly floured surface; punch down to remove air bubbles. Divide dough into 12 pieces. On floured surface, roll each piece into an 8-inch circle. Spoon pizza sauce, cheese, and any desired toppings onto half of each circle. Moisten edge of dough with mixture of 1 egg and 1 teaspoon water. Fold in half; seal edge by pressing with fork. Prick each top; brush with remaining egg mixture. Bake on greased cookie sheets in preheated 375° F oven 30 to 35 minutes or until golden brown. Serve immediately.

Makes 12 calzones.

Pretzels

Like bagels, the best soft pretzels are boiled before they are baked. Try serving these with spicy yellow mustard.

Ingredients

Water	1 cup	**Sugar**	1 tablespoon
Vegetable oil	2 tablespoons	**Bread flour**	3 cups
Salt	½ teaspoon	**Active dry yeast**	2 ¼ teaspoons

Bread Machine Method

Have liquid ingredients at 80° F and all others at room temperature. Place ingredients in pan in the order specified in your owner's manual. Select dough/manual cycle. Do not use the delay timer.

Mixer Method

Combine yeast, 1 cup flour, and other dry ingredients. Combine liquids and heat to 120° to 130° F.

Hand-Held Mixer Method Combine dry mixture and liquid ingredients in mixing bowl on low speed. Beat 2 to 3 minutes on medium speed. By hand, stir in enough remaining flour to make a firm dough. Knead on floured surface 5 to 7 minutes or until smooth and elastic. Use additional flour if necessary. Place dough in lightly oiled bowl and turn to grease top. Cover; let rise until dough tests ripe.

Stand Mixer Method Combine dry mixture and liquid ingredients in mixing bowl with paddle or beaters for 4 minutes on medium speed. Gradually add remaining flour and knead with dough hook(s) 5 to 7 minutes until smooth and elastic. Place dough in lightly oiled bowl and turn to grease top. Cover; let rise until dough tests ripe.

Food Processor Method Put dry mixture in processing bowl with steel blade. While motor is running, add liquid ingredients. Process until mixed. Continue processing, adding remaining flour until dough forms a ball. Place dough in lightly oiled bowl and turn to grease top. Cover; let rise until dough tests ripe.

Shaping and Baking

Turn dough onto lightly floured surface; punch down to remove air bubbles. Divide dough into 4 parts and each part into 3 pieces. Roll into 18-inch ropes. Shape ropes into a circle, overlapping about 4 inches from each end. Twist ends at point of overlap and lay across the opposite edges of circle. Tuck ends under; seal. Place on greased cookie sheet. Let rise until puffy, about 20 minutes.

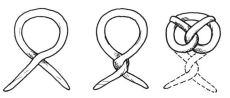

In a 3-quart saucepan, bring 2 quarts water and ⅓ cup baking soda to a boil. Simmer 1 to 2 pretzels 10 seconds on each side. Remove with slotted spoon. Place on greased cookie sheet. Let dry briefly. Brush with 1 slightly beaten egg white; sprinkle with coarse salt or sesame seeds. Bake in preheated 425° F oven 12 minutes.

Makes 12 pretzels.

Challah

This egg-rich braid is traditionally served in Jewish households to begin the Sabbath. Try serving for breakfast with fruit preserves or slice thick and use to make superb French toast.

Ingredients

Water	¼ cup
Milk	¾ cup
Eggs, room temperature	2
Butter, room temperature	2 tablespoons
Salt	2 teaspoons
Sugar	2 tablespoons
Bread flour	3 cups
Active dry yeast	2 ¼ teaspoons

Bread Machine Method

Have liquid ingredients at 80° F and all others at room temperature. Place ingredients in pan in the order specified in your owner's manual. Select dough/manual cycle. Do not use the delay timer.

Mixer Methods

Combine yeast, 1 cup flour, and other dry ingredients. Combine water and milk; heat to 120° to 130° F.

Hand-Held Mixer Method Combine dry mixture, liquid ingredients, and butter in mixing bowl on low speed. Beat 2 to 3 minutes on medium speed. Add eggs; beat 1 minute. By hand, stir in enough remaining flour to make a firm dough. Knead on floured surface 5 to 7 minutes or until smooth and elastic. Use additional flour if necessary. Place dough in lightly oiled bowl and turn to grease top. Cover; let rise until dough tests ripe.

Stand Mixer Method Combine dry mixture, liquid ingredients, and butter in mixing bowl with paddle or beaters for 4 minutes on medium speed. Add eggs; beat 1 minute. Gradually add remaining flour and knead with dough hook(s) 5 to 7 minutes until smooth and elastic. Place dough in lightly oiled bowl and turn to grease top. Cover; let rise until dough tests ripe.

Food Processor Method Put dry mixture in processing bowl with steel blade. While motor is running, add eggs, butter, and liquid ingredients. Process until mixed. Continue processing, adding remaining flour until dough forms a ball. Place dough in lightly oiled bowl and turn to grease top. Cover; let rise until dough test ripe.

Shaping and Baking

Turn dough onto lightly floured surface; punch down to remove air bubbles. Roll or pat into a 12- x 6-inch rectangle. Cut into two 3- x 12-inch strips. Twist the strips together. Place in a 9- x 5-inch greased bread pan or on a greased cookie sheet. Cover; let rise until indentation remains after touching. For a shiny crust, brush with a combination of 1 slightly beaten egg and 1 tablespoon water or milk. Sprinkle with sesame seeds, if desired. Bake in preheated 400° F oven 20 to 25 minutes. Remove from pan; cool.

Makes 1 loaf.

Egg Bread

Ingredients	Small	Medium	Large
Water	¼ cup	¼ cup	¼ cup
Milk	¼ cup	¼ cup	¼ cup
Egg(s), room temperature	1	2	3
Butter, room temperature	1 tablespoon + 1 teaspoon	2 tablespoons	2 tablespoons + 2 teaspoons
Salt	1 ½ teaspoons	2 teaspoons	2 ½ teaspoons
Sugar	1 tablespoon + 1 teaspoon	2 tablespoons	2 tablespoons + 2 teaspoons
Bread flour	2 ¼ cups	3 cups	4 cups
Active dry yeast	1 ½ teaspoons	2 ¼ teaspoons	1 tablespoon

Bread Machine Method

Have liquid ingredients at 80° F and all others at room temperature. Place ingredients in pan in the order specified in your owner's manual. Select basic cycle and medium/normal crust. Do not use the delay timer.

Mixer Methods

Using ingredient amounts listed for medium loaf, combine yeast, 1 cup flour, and other dry ingredients. Combine water and milk; heat to 120° to 130° F.

Hand-Held Mixer Method Combine dry mixture, liquid ingredients, and butter in mixing bowl on low speed. Beat 2 to 3 minutes on medium speed. Add eggs; beat 1 minute. By hand, stir in enough remaining flour to make a firm dough. Knead on floured surface 5 to 7 minutes or until smooth and elastic. Use additional flour if necessary.

Stand Mixer Method Combine dry mixture, liquid ingredients, and butter in mixing bowl with paddle or beaters for 4 minutes on medium speed. Add eggs; beat 1 minute. Gradually add remaining flour and knead with dough hook(s) 5 to 7 minutes until smooth and elastic.

Food Processor Method Put dry mixture in processing bowl with steel blade. While motor is running, add eggs, butter, and liquid ingredients. Process until mixed. Continue processing, adding remaining flour until dough forms a ball.

Rising, Shaping, and Baking

Place dough in lightly oiled bowl and turn to grease top. Cover; let rise until dough tests ripe. Turn dough onto lightly floured surface; punch down to remove air bubbles. Roll or pat into a 14- x 7-inch rectangle. Starting with shorter side, roll up tightly, pressing dough into roll. Pinch edges and ends to seal. Place in greased 9- x 5-inch loaf pan. Cover; let rise until indentation remains after touching. Brush loaf with slightly beaten egg mixed with 1 tablespoon water. Sprinkle with sesame or poppy seeds. Bake in preheated 375° F oven 30 to 40 minutes. Remove from pan; cool.

Makes 1 loaf.

Whole Wheat Cottage Cheese Rolls

The Cottage cheese blends in quickly with the other ingredients, making for light, puffy rolls.

Ingredients

Water	½ cup	**Brown sugar**	¼ cup
Cottage cheese	1 ½ cups	**Baking soda**	½ teaspoon
Eggs, room temperature	2	**Bread flour**	1 ½ cups
Butter, room temperature	2 tablespoons	**Whole wheat flour**	2 cups
Salt	2 teaspoons	**Active dry yeast**	1 tablespoon

Bread Machine Method

Have water and cottage cheese at 80° F and all others at room temperature. Place ingredients in pan in the order specified in your owner's manual. Select dough/manual cycle. Do not use the delay timer.

Mixer Methods

Combine yeast, 1 cup bread flour, and other dry ingredients, except whole wheat flour. Combine water and cottage cheese; heat to 120° to 130° F.

Hand-Held Mixer Method Combine dry mixture, liquid ingredients, and butter in mixing bowl on low speed. Beat 2 to 3 minutes on medium speed. Add eggs; beat 1 minute. By hand, stir in whole wheat flour and enough remaining bread flour to make a firm dough. Knead on floured surface 5 to 7 minutes or until smooth and elastic. Use additional bread flour if necessary. Place dough in lightly oiled bowl and turn to grease top. Cover; let rise until dough tests ripe.

Stand Mixer Method Combine dry mixture, liquid ingredients, and butter in mixing bowl with paddle or beaters for 4 minutes on medium speed. Add eggs; beat 1 minute. Gradually add whole wheat flour and remaining bread flour and knead with dough hook(s) 5 to 7 minutes until smooth and elastic. Place dough in lightly oiled bowl and turn to grease top. Cover; let rise until dough tests ripe.

Food Processor Method Put dry mixture in processing bowl with steel blade. While motor is running, add butter, eggs, and liquid ingredients. Process until mixed. Continue processing, adding whole wheat flour and remaining bread flour until dough forms a ball. Place dough in lightly oiled bowl and turn to grease top. Cover; let rise until dough tests ripe.

Shaping and Baking

Turn dough onto lightly floured surface; punch down to remove air bubbles. Divide dough into 4 parts. Divide each part into 6 pieces. Shape each piece into a smooth ball. Place in two greased 8-inch square pans. Cover; let rise until indentation remains after touching. Bake in preheated 375° F oven 12 to 15 minutes or until tested done. Brush with melted butter. Remove from pans and cool.

Makes 24 rolls.

Cook's Note: Rolls may be made ahead by prebaking in a preheated 400° F oven 15 minutes. Remove from pan; cool. Wrap tightly and freeze for later use. To serve, thaw, then bake in a preheated 425° F oven 7 minutes.

Quick and Easy Croissants

Croissants were first prepared by Viennese bakers to commemorate the end of Ottoman rule. Our simplified version eliminates the need to roll in layer after layer of butter, not to mention extra fat.

Ingredients

Water	½ cup
Evaporated milk	⅓ cup
Butter, room temperature	3 tablespoons
Egg, room temperature	1
Salt	1 ½ teaspoons
Sugar	3 tablespoons
Bread flour	3 cups
Active dry yeast	2 ¼ teaspoons

Bread Machine Method

Have liquid ingredients at 80° F and all others at room temperature. Place ingredients in pan in the order specified in your owner's manual. Select dough/manual cycle. Do not use the delay timer. At the end of the last kneading cycle, press STOP/CLEAR, remove dough and proceed with rising, shaping, and baking instructions.

Mixer Methods

Combine yeast, 1 cup flour, and other dry ingredients. Combine water and milk; heat to 120° to 130° F.

Hand-Held Mixer Method Combine dry mixture, liquid ingredients, and butter in mixing bowl on low speed. Beat 2 to 3 minutes on medium speed. Add egg; beat 1 minute. By hand, stir in enough remaining flour to make a firm dough. Knead on floured surface 5 to 7 minutes or until smooth and elastic. Use additional flour if necessary.

Stand Mixer Method Combine dry mixture, liquid ingredients, and butter in mixing bowl with paddle or beaters for 4 minutes on medium speed. Add egg; beat 1 minute. Gradually add remaining flour and knead with dough hook(s) 5 to 7 minutes until smooth and elastic.

Food Processor Method Put dry mixture in processing bowl with steel blade. While motor is running, add egg, butter, and liquid ingredients. Process until mixed. Continue processing, adding remaining flour until dough forms a ball.

Rising, Shaping, and Baking

Place dough in lightly oiled bowl and turn to grease top. Cover and refrigerate for 2 hours. Place dough on floured surface and knead about 6 times to release air bubbles. Divide into 4 parts. Roll each part into a 14-inch circle. With a sharp knife, cut into 8 pie-shaped wedges. Starting with wide edge, roll each wedge toward the point. Place on ungreased cookie sheets, point side down, and curve into crescent shape. Cover; let rise until indentation remains after touching. Combine 1 slightly beaten egg and 1 tablespoon water; brush croissants with egg mixture. Bake in preheated 350° F oven 15 to 18 minutes or until golden brown. Remove from cookie sheets and cool.

Makes 32 croissants.

Refrigerator Rolls

An excellent recipe for those busy days. Placing the dough in the refrigerator to rise allows you to prepare it one day and bake it the next.

Ingredients

Water	1 cup + 1 tablespoon
Butter, room temperature	2 tablespoons
Salt	1 ½ teaspoons
Sugar	1 tablespoon + 1 ½ teaspoons
Bread flour	3 ½ cups
Active dry yeast	2 ¼ teaspoons

Bread Machine Method

Have water at 80° F and all other ingredients at room temperature. Place ingredients in pan in the order specified in your owner's manual. Select dough/manual cycle. At the end of the kneading cycle press STOP/CLEAR, remove dough and proceed with rising, shaping, and baking instructions.

Mixer Methods

Combine yeast, 1 cup flour, and other dry ingredients. Heat water to 120° to 130° F.

Hand-Held Mixer Method Combine dry mixture, water, and butter in mixing bowl on low speed. Beat 2 to 3 minutes on medium speed. By hand, stir in enough remaining flour to make a firm dough. Knead on floured surface 5 to 7 minutes or until smooth and elastic. Use additional flour if necessary.

Stand Mixer Method Combine dry mixture, water, and butter in mixing bowl with paddle or beaters for 4 minutes on medium speed. Gradually add remaining flour and knead with dough hook(s) 5 to 7 minutes until smooth and elastic.

Food Processor Method Put dry mixture in processing bowl with steel blade. While motor is running, add water, and butter. Process until mixed. Continue processing, adding remaining flour until dough forms a ball.

Rising, Shaping, and Baking

Place dough in lightly oiled bowl and turn to grease top. Cover with plastic wrap or foil. Refrigerate 6 to 12 hours. While the dough is chilling, punch down several times. Remove dough from refrigerator, punch down, and allow to rest 10 minutes before shaping. Divide into 4 parts. Divide each fourth into 4 pieces and shape into rolls. Place rolls 2 to 3 inches apart on greased cookie sheet. Cover; let rise at room temperature until indentation remains when touched. Combine 1 egg and 1 tablespoon water; gently brush rolls. Sprinkle with sesame or poppy seeds, if desired. Bake in preheated 400° F oven 8 to 10 minutes. Remove from cookie sheet. Serve warm or cold.

Makes 16 rolls.

How to Shape My Rolls

Round Pan Rolls Flour hands and break off Ping-Pong ball-sized pieces of dough. Form into smooth balls and place in pan so sides just touch.

Cloverleaf Rolls Flour hands and break off large marble-sized pieces of dough. Form into smooth balls and place 3 in each greased muffin cup.

Parker House Rolls Flour hands and break off walnut-sized pieces of dough. Flatten with palm of hand into an oval shape. Brush with melted butter. With a knife, crease each lengthwise slightly off center. Fold ovals over to make half circles; press to seal. Place on greased cookie sheet.

Crescent Rolls Roll dough out into a circle ¼-inch thick. Cut circle into 8 wedges. Starting at the wide end, roll each wedge toward the point. Place point side down on greased cookie sheet.

Fan-Shaped Rolls Roll dough into a large rectangle about ¼-inch thick. Cut into 1½-inch strips. Stack 5 strips together; cut into 1½-inch pieces and place cut side up in a greased muffin cup.

Finger Rolls Flour hands and break off walnut-sized pieces of dough. Shape each into a roll about 4-inches long. Place on greased pan so that sides just touch.

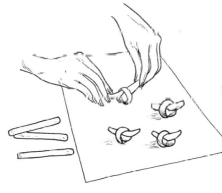

Bow Knots Flour hands and break off walnut-sized pieces of dough. Shape each into a 9-inch coil. Tie in loose knots. Place on greased cookie sheet.

Swirls Flour hands and break off large walnut-sized pieces of dough. Roll each into a 10-inch rope. Loosely coil each row on greased cookie sheet.

S' Flour hands and break off large walnut-sized pieces of dough. Roll each into a 10-inch rope. Form each rope into the letter "S" on greased cookie sheet.

Bunnies Flour hands and divide dough into 9 balls. Roll each into an 18-inch rope. Cut 10 inches for the body, 5 inches for the head, and 1 inch each for the tail and ears. Coil rolls for head and body; piece together on greased cookie sheet. Form ears and tail; attach to bunny.

Chicks Flour hands and divide dough into 9 balls. Roll each ball into a 14-inch rope. Tie a loose knot, leaving one end short. Pinch the short end to shape a head and beak. Flatten other end for the tail; snip end of tail for fanned effect. Place on greased cookie sheet.

Chapter 6
Loaves For Celebration

Turn your kitchen into a hub of activity in preparation for the holidays. The warm fragrance of yeast dough will touch the spirit of anyone who comes near your kitchen. Soon the sense of festivity will be upon you, your family, and your friends. You will have fresh baked goods to serve or give as gifts. Be sure to refer to Storing Dough and Bread in Chapter 1, so you can prepare early. Dividing your baking activities into steps, making the dough ahead of time and refrigerating or freezing it, allows you to fit holiday baking into an already busy schedule.

You will be amazed at the ease of making Kolaches when the dough is already prepared and all you have to do is roll them out and fill them before baking. Dough for Stollen can also be prepared ahead. In fact, the Stollen can even be shaped before freezing. Remember, the thawing time is not really your working time. Hot Cross Buns will be ready for the oven in the early morning if they are allowed to thaw in the refrigerator overnight.

Celebrations bring families and friends together to enjoy fellowship and fine foods. Loaves for Celebrations includes the special breads you will want to share at these times.

Rich Refrigerator Rolls

So you thought you had no time to bake? Well, think again with these refrigerator rolls. The dough is prepared before going to bed and rises slowly in a cold refrigerator. All you have to do the next day is shape and bake these rolls.

Ingredients

Water	1 cup
Butter, room temperature	3 tablespoons
Egg, room temperature	1
Salt	1 teaspoon
Sugar	¼ cup
Bread flour	3 ½ cups
Active dry yeast	2 ¼ teaspoons

Bread Machine Method

Have water at 80° F and all other ingredients at room temperature. Place ingredients in pan in the order specified in your owner's manual. Select dough/manual cycle. Do not use the delay timer. At the end of the last kneading cycle, press STOP/CLEAR, remove dough and proceed with rising, shaping, and baking instructions.

Mixer Methods

Using ingredient amounts listed for medium loaf, combine yeast, 1 cup flour, and other dry ingredients. Heat water to 120° to 130° F.

Hand-Held Mixer Method Combine dry mixture, water, and butter in mixing bowl on low speed. Beat 2 to 3 minutes on medium speed. Add egg; beat 1 minute. By hand, stir in enough remaining flour to make a firm dough. Knead on floured surface 5 to 7 minutes or until smooth and elastic. Use additional flour if necessary.

Stand Mixer Method Combine dry mixture, water, and butter in mixing bowl with paddle or beaters for 4 minutes on medium speed. Add egg; beat 1 minute. Gradually add remaining flour and knead with dough hook(s) 5 to 7 minutes until smooth and elastic.

Food Processor Method Put dry mixture in processing bowl with steel blade. While motor is running, add water, butter, and egg. Process until mixed. Continue processing, adding remaining flour until dough forms a ball.

Rising, Shaping, and Baking

Place dough in lightly oiled bowl and turn to grease top. Cover with plastic wrap or foil. Refrigerate 6 to 12 hours. The dough will need to be punched down in a couple of hours. Remove dough from refrigerator, punch down, and allow to rest 10 minutes before shaping. Divide dough into 4 parts. Divide each fourth into 4 pieces and shape into rolls. Place rolls 2 to 3 inches apart on greased cookie sheets. Cover; let rise at room temperature until indentation remains when touched. Combine 1 egg and 1 tablespoon water; gently brush onto rolls. Sprinkle with sesame or poppy seeds, if desired. Bake in preheated 400° F oven 8 to 10 minutes. Remove from cookie sheets. Serve warm or cold.

Makes 16 rolls.

Danish Yeast Rolls

Serve these buttery-rich Danish sweet rolls to turn an ordinary occasion into a special event.

Ingredients

Milk	1 cup
Butter, room temperature	¾ cup
Egg yolks, room temperature	3
Salt	1 ½ teaspoons
Sugar	¼ cup
Bread flour	3 cups
Active dry yeast	2 ¼ teaspoons

Bread Machine Method

Have milk at 80° F and all other ingredients at room temperature. Place ingredients in pan in the order specified in your owner's manual. Select dough/manual cycle. Do not use the delay timer.

Mixer Methods

Combine yeast, 1 cup flour, and other dry ingredients. Heat milk to 120° to 130° F.

Hand-Held Mixer Method Combine dry mixture, milk, and butter in mixing bowl on low speed. Beat 2 to 3 minutes on medium speed. Add egg yolks; beat 1 minute. By hand, stir in enough remaining flour to make a firm dough. Knead on floured surface 5 to 7 minutes or until smooth and elastic. Add additional flour if necessary. Place dough in lightly oiled bowl and turn to grease top. Cover; let rise until dough tests ripe.

Stand Mixer Method Combine dry mixture, milk, and butter in mixing bowl with paddle or beaters for 4 minutes on medium speed. Add egg yolks; beat 1 minute. Gradually add flour and knead with dough hook(s) 5 to 7 minutes until smooth and elastic. Place dough in lightly oiled bowl and turn to grease top. Cover; let rise until dough tests ripe.

Food Processor Method Put dry mixture in processing bowl with steel blade. While motor is running, add milk, butter, and egg yolks. Process until mixed. Continue processing, adding remaining flour until dough forms a ball. Place dough in lightly oiled bowl and turn to grease top. Cover; let rise until dough tests ripe.

Shaping and Baking

Divide dough into 2 parts. Refrigerate half of dough until ready to use. On lightly floured surface, roll half into a 12- x 9-inch rectangle. Brush with 1 tablespoon melted butter. Sprinkle with 2 tablespoons sugar and ¼ cup coconut. Starting with longer side, roll up tightly. Pinch edge to seal. Cut into 12 slices. Place on greased cookie sheets. Repeat directions with remaining half of dough. Cover; let rise until indentation remains when touched. Bake in preheated 350° F oven 20 to 25 minutes. Remove from cookie sheets. Drizzle with powdered sugar glaze (page 91); serve warm.

Makes 24 rolls.

Sticky Buns

A quick and easy recipe to prepare in the morning or when unexpected company drops in for coffee.

Ingredients

Water	¼ cup	**Salt**	1 teaspoon
Milk	½ cup	**Sugar**	2 tablespoons
Butter, room temperature	2 tablespoons	**Bread flour**	3 cups
Egg, room temperature	1	**Active dry yeast**	2 ¼ teaspoons

Topping

Butter, room temperature	2 tablespoons	**Sugar**	2 tablespoons
Packed brown sugar	¼ cup	**Cinnamon**	2 teaspoons

Bread Machine Method

Have liquid ingredients at 80° F and all others at room temperature. Place ingredients in pan in the order specified in your owner's manual. Select dough/manual cycle. Do not use the delay timer.

Mixer Methods

Combine yeast, 1 cup flour, and other dry ingredients. Combine water and milk; heat to 120° to 130° F.

Hand-Held Mixer Method Combine dry mixture, liquid ingredients, and butter in mixing bowl on low speed. Beat 2 to 3 minutes on medium speed. Add egg; beat 1 minute. By hand, stir in enough remaining flour to make a firm dough. Knead on floured surface 5 to 7 minutes or until smooth and elastic. Add additional flour if necessary. Place dough in lightly oiled bowl and turn to grease top. Cover; let rise until dough tests ripe.

Stand Mixer Method Combine dry mixture, liquid ingredients, and butter in mixing bowl with paddle or beaters for 4 minutes on medium speed. Add egg; beat 1 minute. Gradually add remaining flour and knead with dough hook(s) 5 to 7 minutes until smooth and elastic. Place dough in lightly oiled bowl and turn to grease top. Cover; let rise until dough tests ripe.

Food Processor Method Put dry mixture in processing bowl with steel blade. While motor is running, add butter, egg, and liquid ingredients. Process until mixed. Continue processing, adding remaining flour until dough forms a ball. Place dough in lightly oiled bowl and turn to grease top. Cover; let rise until dough tests ripe.

Shaping and Baking

Turn dough onto lightly floured surface; punch down to remove air bubbles. Roll or pat into a 15- x 12-inch rectangle. Spread with 2 tablespoons softened butter. Mix together dry topping ingredients and sprinkle onto dough. Starting with shorter side, roll up tightly. Pinch edges to seal. Cut into 12 slices. Place in greased 13- x 9-inch cake pan. Cover; let rise until indentation remains when touched. Bake in preheated 375° F oven 20 to 25 minutes. Remove from pan; cool.

Makes 12 rolls.

Yeast Pie Crust

Are you frustrated rolling out difficult-to-work short doughs? Then try our flaky, simple-to-use yeast version.

Ingredients

Water	½ cup	**Salt**	1 teaspoon
Milk	2 tablespoons	**Sugar**	¼ cup
Vegetable oil	¼ cup	**Bread flour**	3 cups
Egg, room temperature	1	**Active dry yeast**	2 ¼ teaspoons

Streusel Topping

Brown sugar	2 tablespoons	**Cinnamon**	1 teaspoon
Flour	2 tablespoons	**Butter**	2 tablespoons

Bread Machine Method

Have liquid ingredients at 80° F and all others at room temperature. Place ingredients in pan in the order specified in your owner's manual. Select dough/manual cycle. Do not use the delay timer.

Mixer Methods

Using ingredient amounts listed for medium loaf, combine yeast, 1 cup flour, and other dry ingredients. Combine water, milk, and oil; heat to 120° to 130° F.

Hand-Held Mixer Method Combine dry mixture and liquid ingredients in mixing bowl on low speed. Beat 2 to 3 minutes on medium speed. Add egg; beat 1 minute. By hand, stir in enough remaining flour to make a firm dough. Knead on floured surface 5 to 7 minutes or until smooth and elastic. Add additional flour if necessary. Place dough in lightly oiled bowl and turn to grease top. Cover, let rise until dough tests ripe.

Stand Mixer Method Combine dry mixture and liquid ingredients in mixing bowl with paddle or beaters for 4 minutes on medium speed. Add egg; beat 1 minute. Gradually add remaining flour and knead with dough hook(s) 5 to 7 minutes until smooth and elastic. Place dough in lightly oiled bowl and turn to grease top. Cover; let rise until dough tests ripe.

Food Processor Method Put dry mixture in processing bowl with steel blade. While motor is running, add egg and liquid ingredients. Process until mixed. Continue processing, adding remaining flour until dough forms a ball. Place dough in lightly oiled bowl and turn to grease top. Cover; let rise until dough tests ripe.

Shaping and Baking

Turn dough onto lightly floured surface; punch down to remove air bubbles. Divide into 2 pieces. Roll one piece into a 12-inch circle to fit a 10-inch pie plate. Press into the pie plate; flute edges. Pour prepared pie filling into shell. Combine Streusel Topping ingredients and crumble over filling. Bake in preheated 400° F oven for 15 minutes. Reduce oven temperature to 325° F and bake additional 20 to 25 minutes. Serve warm or cold.

Makes 2 pie crusts.

Cook's Note: Remaining portion of dough may be frozen for later use. See Storing Dough and Bread in Chapter 1.

Kolache

These wonderful, Eastern European sweet buns are a perennial favorite of ours.

Ingredients

Water	¼ cup
Milk	¾ cup
Butter, room temperature	¼ cup
Egg, room temperature	1
Salt	1 teaspoon
Sugar	¼ cup
Bread flour	3 ½ cups
Active dry yeast	2 ¼ teaspoons

Bread Machine Method

Have liquid ingredients at 80° F and all others at room temperature. Place ingredients in pan in the order specified in your owner's manual. Select dough/manual cycle. Do not use the delay timer.

Mixer Methods

Combine yeast, 1 cup flour, and other dry ingredients. Combine water and milk; heat to 120° to 130° F.

Hand-Held Mixer Method Combine dry mixture, liquid ingredients, and butter in mixing bowl on low speed. Beat 2 to 3 minutes on medium speed. Add egg; beat 1 minute. By hand, stir in enough remaining flour to make a firm dough. Knead on floured surface 5 to 7 minutes or until smooth and elastic. Add additional flour if necessary. Place dough in lightly oiled bowl and turn to grease top. Cover; let rise until dough tests ripe.

Stand Mixer Method Combine dry mixture, liquid ingredients, and butter in mixing bowl with paddle or beaters for 4 minutes on medium speed. Add egg; beat 1 minute. Gradually add remaining flour and knead with dough hook(s) 5 to 7 minutes until smooth and elastic. Place dough in lightly oiled bowl and turn to grease top. Cover; let rise until dough tests ripe.

Food Processor Method Put dry mixture in processing bowl with steel blade. While motor is running, add butter, egg, and liquid ingredients. Process until mixed. Continue processing, adding remaining flour until dough forms a ball. Place dough in lightly oiled bowl and turn to grease top. Cover; let rise until dough tests ripe.

Shaping and Baking

Turn dough onto lightly floured surface; punch down to remove air bubbles. Divide into 2 parts. On lightly floured surface, roll each half into a 12-inch square. Cut each square into nine 4-inch squares. Spoon desired filling into center of each square. Fold one corner to the center. Moisten corner of dough with water. Fold opposite corner over and seal. Place on greased cookie sheets. Cover; let rise until indentation remains after touching. Brush with melted butter. Bake in preheated 375° F oven 12 to 15 minutes. Remove from cookie sheets. Serve warm or cold.

Makes 18 rolls.

Prune Orange Kolache Filling

Prune puree	¾ cup
Chopped nuts	⅓ cup
Orange marmalade	⅓ cup
Lemon juice	1 teaspoon

Cream Cheese Raisin Kolache Filling

Cream cheese	2 (3 ounces) packages
Sugar	2 tablespoons
Egg	1
Lemon zest	1 teaspoon
Golden raisins	¼ cup

Apricot Almond Kolache Filling

Cooked apricot halves, chopped	1 cup
Brown sugar	⅓ cup
Chopped almonds	⅓ cup
Cinnamon	½ teaspoon

Combine all filling ingredients; mix until smooth with mixer or blender. Use about 2 to 3 teaspoons of filling for each Kolache.

Spring cannot be too far off once hot cross buns appear on bakery and supermarket shelves. Ground cloves and nutmeg give these sweet buns their distinct, good flavor.

Ingredients

Milk	½ cup
Water	½ cup
Butter, room temperature	¼ cup
Egg, room temperature	1
Lemon zest	2 tablespoons
Cinnamon	1 teaspoon
Ground cloves	¼ teaspoon
Ground nutmeg	¼ teaspoon
Salt	1 teaspoon
Sugar	¼ cup
Bread flour	3 ½ cups
Active dry yeast	2 ¼ teaspoons
Dried currants	¾ cup

Bread Machine Method

Have liquid ingredients at 80° F and all others at room temperature. Place ingredients in pan in the order specified in your owner's manual. Select dough/manual cycle. Currants can be added 5 minutes before the end of the last kneading. Do not use the delay timer.

Mixer Methods

Combine yeast, 1 cup flour, and other dry ingredients, except currants. Combine milk and water; heat to 120° to 130° F.

Hand-Held Mixer Method Combine dry mixture, liquid ingredients, and butter in mixing bowl on low speed. Beat 2 to 3 minutes on medium speed. Add egg; beat 1 minute. By hand, stir in currants and enough remaining flour to make a firm dough. Knead on floured surface 5 to 7 minutes or until smooth and elastic. Add additional flour if necessary. Place dough in lightly oiled bowl and turn to grease top. Cover; let rise until dough tests ripe.

Stand Mixer Method Combine dry mixture, liquid ingredients, and butter in mixing bowl with paddle or beaters for 4 minutes on medium speed. Add egg; beat 1 minute. Gradually add currants and remaining flour and knead with dough hook(s) 5 to 7 minutes until smooth and elastic. Place dough in lightly oiled bowl and turn to grease top. Cover; let rise until dough tests ripe.

Food Processor Method Put dry mixture in processing bowl with steel blade. While motor is running, add liquid ingredients, butter, and egg. Process until mixed. Continue processing, adding remaining flour until dough forms a ball. Add currants; pulse just until mixed. Place dough in lightly oiled bowl and turn to grease top. Cover; let rise until dough tests ripe.

Shaping and Baking

Turn dough onto lightly floured surface; punch down to remove air bubbles. Divide dough into 3 parts. Divide each third into 6 pieces. Shape each piece into a smooth ball. Place on greased cookie sheet, sides touching. Cover; let rise until indentation remains after touching. Combine 1 egg yolk and 1 tablespoon water; brush buns. Bake in preheated

375° F oven for 10 to 12 minutes. Remove from cookie sheet; cool. Frost with Powdered Sugar Glaze (see below).

Makes 18 rolls

Powdered Sugar Glaze

Powdered sugar	1 cup
Vanilla	½ teaspoon
Water	3 to 4 teaspoons

Combine all ingredients in small mixing bowl; beat until smooth.

Stollen

Holiday bread baking plays an important role in many cultures. Over the years, the following German Christmas bread has crossed over many cultural boundaries and today appears on many families' holiday tables.

Ingredients

Rich Refrigerator Rolls (page 84)	
Chopped candied cherries	⅓ cup
Chopped citron	3 tablespoons
Raisins	3 tablespoons
Chopped walnuts or pecans	3 tablespoons

Bread Machine Method
Add the dried fruit and nuts to the Rich Refrigerator Rolls (page 84) 5 minutes before the end of the last kneading cycle.

Mixer Methods
Hand-Held and Stand Mixer Methods Follow directions for Rich Refrigerator Rolls (page 84), adding the dried fruit and nuts with the remaining flour to make a firm dough.
Food Processor Method Add the fruit and dried nuts after dough has formed ball, pulse just until mixed.

Shaping and Baking
On lightly floured surface, roll or pat dough into a 14- x 8-inch oval. Spread with 1 tablespoon softened butter. Fold in half lengthwise and curve into a crescent shape. Press folded edge firmly to partially seal. Place on greased cookie sheet. Cover; let rise until indentation remains when touched. Bake in preheated 350° F oven for 25 to 30 minutes. Remove from cookie sheet; cool. Drizzle with Powdered Sugar Glaze (see above) and garnish with additional cherries and nuts, if desired.

Makes 1 stollen.

Doughnuts

Years ago, housewives and mothers treated their families to fried cakes and pastries like these extraordinary, risen doughnuts.

Ingredients

Milk	½ cup
Water	¼ cup
Vegetable oil	¼ cup
Egg, room temperature	1
Salt	1 teaspoon
Sugar	¼ cup
Bread flour	3 cups
Active dry yeast	2 ¼ teaspoons

Bread Machine Method

Have liquid ingredients at 80° F and all others at room temperature. Place ingredients in pan in the order specified in your owner's manual. Select dough/manual cycle. Do not use the delay timer.

Mixer Methods

Combine yeast, 1 cup flour, and other dry ingredients. Combine milk, water, and oil; heat to 120° to 130° F.

Hand-Held Mixer Method Combine dry mixture and liquid ingredients in mixing bowl on low speed. Beat 2 to 3 minutes on medium speed. Add egg; beat 1 minute. By hand, stir in enough remaining flour to make a firm dough. Knead on floured surface 5 to 7 minutes or until smooth and elastic. Add additional flour if necessary. Place dough in lightly oiled bowl and turn to grease top. Cover; let rise until dough tests ripe.

Stand Mixer Method Combine dry mixture and liquid ingredients in mixing bowl with paddle or beaters for 4 minutes on medium speed. Add egg; beat 1 minute. Gradually add remaining flour and knead with dough hook(s) 5 to 7 minutes until smooth and elastic. Place dough in lightly oiled bowl and turn to grease top. Cover; let rise until dough tests ripe.

Food Processor Method Put dry mixture in processing bowl with steel blade. While motor is running, add egg and liquid ingredients. Process until mixed. Continue processing, adding remaining flour until dough forms a ball. Place dough in lightly oiled bowl and turn to grease top. Cover; let rise until dough tests ripe.

Shaping and Baking

Turn dough onto lightly floured surface; punch down to remove air bubbles. Divide dough into 2 parts. On lightly floured surface, roll each half into a 12- x 6-inch rectangle. Cut with 2 ½-inch doughnut cutter. Place on lightly floured cookie sheets. Cover; let rise until indentation remains after touching. In large heavy pot, heat 4 inches vegetable oil to 400° F. Fry doughnuts a few at a time, turning once, until golden brown. Drain on absorbent paper towels. Glaze or shake in a paper sack with sugar.

Makes 24 doughnuts.

Croutes

You will describe these little pies as versatile and delicious. They are sensational served warm with your favorite cheese, sausage, or vegetable filling.

Ingredients

Water	1 cup	**Sugar**	2 tablespoons
Butter, room temperature	½ cup	**Bread flour**	3 ½ cups
Salt	1 teaspoon	**Active dry yeast**	2 ¼ teaspoons

Bread Machine Method

Have water at 80° F and all other ingredients at room temperature. Place ingredients in pan in the order specified in your owner's manual. Select dough/manual cycle. Do not use the delay timer.

Mixer Methods

Combine yeast, 1 cup flour, and other dry ingredients. Heat water to 120° to 130° F.

Hand-Held Mixer Method Combine dry mixture, water, and butter in mixing bowl on low speed. Beat 2 to 3 minutes on medium speed. By hand, stir in enough remaining flour to make a firm dough. Knead on floured surface 5 to 7 minutes or until smooth and elastic. Add additional flour if necessary. Place dough in lightly oiled bowl and turn to grease top. Cover; let rise until dough tests ripe.

Stand Mixer Method Combine dry mixture, water, and butter in mixing bowl with paddle or beaters for 4 minutes on medium speed. Gradually add remaining flour and knead with dough hook(s) 5 to 7 minutes until smooth and elastic. Place dough in lightly oiled bowl and turn to grease top. Cover; let rise until dough tests ripe.

Food Processor Method Put dry mixture in processing bowl with steel blade. While motor is running, add water and butter. Process until mixed. Continue processing, adding remaining flour until dough forms a ball. Place dough in lightly oiled bowl and turn to grease top. Cover; let rise until dough tests ripe.

Shaping and Baking

Turn dough onto lightly floured surface; punch down to remove air bubbles. Divide dough into 6 parts. Divide each part into 5 pieces. Pat each piece into a 4-inch circle; place on greased cookie sheet. Spoon about 1 tablespoon filling on each circle. Fold the circle in half and seal edges by pressing with fingers, then with a fork. Brush tops with beaten egg. Bake in preheated 400° F oven for 12 to 15 minutes. Remove from cookie sheet. Serve warm.

Makes 30 Croutes.

Cheese Filling for 15 Croutes		Sausage Cheese Filling for 15 Croutes	
Egg	1	**Bulk pork sausage,**	½ pound
Ricotta cheese	½ cup	browned and drained	
Grated Parmesan cheese	2 tablespoons	**Grated Swiss cheese**	¾ cup
Chopped parsley	2 teaspoons	**Prepared mustard**	2 teaspoons
Shredded mozzarella	1 cup	**Prepared horseradish**	1 tablespoon
cheese			

Strawberry Almond Bread

Strawberry Almond Bread is an excellent tasting and attractive tea bread—contributed to our Baker's Collection by Pam Phillips of Manitowoc, Wisconsin.

Ingredients	Small	Medium	Large
Water	2 tablespoons	5 tablespoons	¼ cup
Sour cream	3 tablespoons	¼ cup	5 tablespoons
Sliced fresh strawberries	¾ cup	1 cup	1 ¼ cups
Vegetable oil	1 tablespoon	2 tablespoons	3 tablespoons
Salt	1 teaspoon	1 ½ teaspoons	2 teaspoons
Sugar	2 tablespoons	3 tablespoons	¼ cup
Slivered almonds	¼ cup	⅓ cup	½ cup
Bread flour	2 ¼ cups	3 cups	4 cups
Active dry yeast	1 ½ teaspoons	2 ¼ teaspoons	1 tablespoon

Bread Machine Method

Have liquid ingredients at 80° F and all others at room temperature. Place ingredients in pan in the order specified in your owner's manual. Select basic cycle and medium/normal crust. Slivered almonds can be added 5 minutes before the end of the last kneading. Do not use the delay timer.

Mixer Methods

Using ingredient amounts listed for medium loaf, combine yeast, 1 cup flour, and other dry ingredients, except almonds. Combine water, sour cream, strawberries, and oil; heat to 120° to 130° F.

Hand-Held Mixer Method Combine dry mixture and liquid ingredients in mixing bowl on low speed. Beat 2 to 3 minutes on medium speed. By hand, stir in slivered almonds and enough remaining flour to make a firm dough. Knead on floured surface 5 to 7 minutes or until smooth and elastic. Add additional flour if necessary.

Stand Mixer Method Combine dry mixture and liquid ingredients in mixing bowl with paddle or beaters for 4 minutes on medium speed. Gradually add slivered almonds and remaining flour and knead with dough hook(s) 5 to 7 minutes until smooth and elastic.

Food Processor Method Put dry mixture in processing bowl with steel blade. While motor is running, add liquid ingredients. Process until mixed. Continue processing, adding remaining flour until dough forms a ball. Add slivered almonds; pulse just until mixed.

Rising, Shaping, and Baking

Place dough in lightly oiled bowl and turn to grease top. Cover; let rise until dough tests ripe. Turn dough onto lightly floured surface; punch down to remove air bubbles. Roll or pat into a 14- x 7-inch rectangle. Starting with shorter side, roll up tightly, pressing dough into roll. Pinch edges and ends to seal. Place in greased 9- x 5-inch loaf pan. Cover; let rise until indentation remains after touching. Bake in preheated 375° F oven 30 to 40 minutes. Remove from pan; cool.

Cook's Note: If more strawberry flavor is desired, substitute strawberry-flavored drink mix for the sugar called for in the recipe.

Makes 1 loaf.

Cardamom Bread

Cardamom, a rich aromatic spice, has been highly regarded by bakers for centuries. This Baker's Collection recipe was contributed by an avid cook and baker, Phyllis Simon of Park Ridge, Illinois.

Ingredients	Small	Medium	Large
Water	1 tablespoon	—	2 tablespoons
Milk	½ cup	¾ cup	1 cup
Butter, room temperature	2 tablespoons	3 tablespoons	¼ cup
Egg, room temperature	1	1	1
Salt	¼ teaspoon	½ teaspoon	¾ teaspoon
Sugar	2 tablespoons	3 tablespoons	¼ cup
Ground cardamom	½ teaspoon	¾ teaspoon	1 teaspoon
Bread flour	2 ¼ cups	3 cups	4 cups
Active dry yeast	1 ½ teaspoons	2 ¼ teaspoons	1 tablespoon

Bread Machine Method

Have liquid ingredients at 80° F and all others at room temperature. Place ingredients in pan in the order specified in your owner's manual. Select basic cycle and medium/normal crust. Do not use the delay timer.

Mixer Methods

Using ingredient amounts listed for medium loaf, combine yeast, 1 cup flour, and other dry ingredients. Combine water and milk; heat to 120° to 130° F.

Hand-Held Mixer Method Combine dry mixture, liquid ingredients, and butter in mixing bowl on low speed. Beat 2 to 3 minutes on medium speed. Add egg; beat 1 minute. By hand, stir in enough remaining flour to make a firm dough. Knead on floured surface 5 to 7 minutes or until smooth and elastic. Add additional flour if necessary.

Stand Mixer Method Combine dry mixture, liquid ingredients, and butter in mixing bowl with paddle or beaters for 4 minutes on medium speed. Add egg; beat 1 minute. Gradually add remaining flour and knead with dough hook(s) 5 to 7 minutes until smooth and elastic.

Food Processor Method Put dry mixture in processing bowl with steel blade. While motor is running, add butter, egg, and liquid ingredients. Process until mixed. Continue processing, adding remaining flour until dough forms a ball.

Rising, Shaping, and Baking

Place dough in lightly oiled bowl and turn to grease top. Cover; let rise until dough tests ripe. Turn dough onto lightly floured surface; punch down to remove air bubbles. Divide dough into 3 parts. Roll each piece into a 16-inch rope; line up ropes one inch apart on a greased cookie sheet. Braid loosely; pinch ends together and tuck under. Cover; let rise until indentation remains when touched. Brush with milk and sprinkle with 1 tablespoon sugar. Bake in preheated 375° F oven 20 to 25 minutes.

Makes 1 loaf.

Pineapple Cheese Coffee Cake

Phyllis Simon of Park Ridge, Illinois, has another surefire winner to add to the Baker's Collection.

Ingredients

Sour cream	½ cup
Butter, room temperature	3 tablespoons
Eggs, room temperature	2
Vanilla	1 teaspoon
Sugar	3 tablespoons
Bread flour	3 cups
Active dry yeast	2 ¼ teaspoons

Bread Machine Method

Have liquid ingredients at 80° F and all others at room temperature. Place ingredients in pan in the order specified in your owner's manual. Select dough/manual cycle. Do not use the delay timer.

Mixer Methods

Combine yeast, 1 cup flour, and sugar. Heat sour cream to 120° to 130° F.

Hand-Held Mixer Method Combine dry mixture, sour cream, and butter in mixing bowl on low speed. Beat 2 to 3 minutes on medium speed. Add eggs and vanilla; beat 1 minute. By hand, stir in enough remaining flour to make a firm dough. Knead on floured surface 5 to 7 minutes or until smooth and elastic. Add additional flour if necessary. Place dough in lightly oiled bowl and turn to grease top. Cover; let rise until dough tests ripe.

Stand Mixer Method Combine dry mixture, sour cream, and butter in mixing bowl with paddle or beaters for 4 minutes on medium speed. Add egg and vanilla; beat 1 minute. Gradually add remaining flour and knead with dough hook(s) 5 to 7 minutes until smooth and elastic. Place dough in lightly oiled bowl and turn to grease top. Cover; let rise until dough tests ripe.

Food Processor Method Put dry mixture in processing bowl with steel blade. While motor is running, add butter, egg, vanilla, and sour cream. Process until mixed. Continue processing, adding remaining flour until dough forms a ball. Place dough in lightly oiled bowl and turn to grease top. Cover; let rise until dough tests ripe.

Shaping and Baking

Turn dough onto lightly floured surface; punch down to remove air bubbles. Divide dough into two unequal pieces (one, ⅓ of dough and one, ⅔ of dough). Roll out larger piece on a floured surface to a 10- x 14-inch rectangle. Place in greased 9- x 13-inch pan; pressing up sides. Spread with Pineapple Cheese Filling. Roll out remaining dough to a 5- x 12-inch strip. Cut into five 1- x 12-inch strips. Lay strips lengthwise over filling. Fold down sides of dough to hold strips in place. Cover; let rise until indentation remains when touched. Bake in preheated 350° F oven 30 to 35 minutes. Cool in pan. Drizzle with Pineapple Icing.

Makes 1 coffee cake.

Pineapple Cheese Filling

Crushed pineapple, drained (reserve juice)	1 (8 ½ ounce) can
Cream cheese, room temperature	1 (8 ounce) package
Egg, room temperature	1
Sugar	1 tablespoon
Salt	⅛ teaspoon

To prepare filling, cream all ingredients together.

Pineapple Icing

Powdered sugar	1 ¼ cups
Pineapple juice (reserved)	3 tablespoons

Add pineapple juice to powdered sugar and stir together until smooth. If the icing is too thin, add more powdered sugar; too thick, add more pineapple juice.

Hand-Held Mixer, Stand Mixer, and Food Processor Methods

Crust is too thick:
- Decrease the flour amount.
- Lengthen the rising time using the ripe test.
- Use a higher oven temperature.

Baked loaf crumbles easily:
- Increase the mixing time.
- Decrease the flour amount.
- Make sure the rising place is not over 90° F.
- Use the ripe test to prevent over-rising.
- Use a higher oven temperature.

Bread has sour taste:
- Make sure the rising place is not over 90° F.
- Use the ripe test to prevent over-rising.

Dough does not rise:
- Use thermometer for accurate liquid temperature.
- Decrease the flour amount.
- Use oven for a rising place.
- Check activity of yeast.

Bread has dark streaks:
- Increase the mixing and kneading times.
- Use less oil to grease rising bowl.
- Be sure dough is covered during rising time.

Bread has holes in it:
- Completely press air out of dough before shaping.
- Use the ripe test to prevent over-rising.

Bread is doughy on bottom:
- Immediately after baking, remove from pans and cool on racks.

Bread has excessive break on side:
- Decrease oven temperature.
- Use the ripe test to be sure dough has risen enough before baking.
- Roll dough tightly and seal edges securely.

Top of loaf cracks:
- Do not cool bread in a draft.
- Decrease flour amount.
- Increase kneading time to develop the gluten better.

Bread doesn't rise in oven:
- Make sure the rising place is not over 90° F.
- Use the ripe test to prevent over-rising.

Bread is heavy and compact:
- Decrease flour amount.
- Use the ripe test to be sure dough has risen enough before baking.
- Certain flours, such as whole wheat and rye, create heavier products than white flour.

Bread is wet inside and coarse grained:
- Use an instant-read thermometer to be certain the bread is completely baked.
- Use the ripe test to be sure dough has risen enough before baking.

Bread does not brown on sides:
- Bright pans reflect heat away from sides; choose dark pans.
- Do not overcrowd the oven.

Bread smells and tastes of yeast:
- Use the ripe test to prevent over-rising.
- Make sure the rising place is not over 90° F.

Bread is dry and has a coarse grain:
- Decrease amount of flour.
- Increase kneading time to develop the gluten better.
- Use the ripe test to prevent over-rising.
- Use a higher oven temperature.

Bread falls in oven:
- Use the ripe test to prevent over-rising.

Bread Machine Method

Crust is too thick:
- Remove bread from machine immediately after bake cycle is completed.

Bread collapses during baking:
- Use a thermometer to accurately measure the liquid temperature.
- Use less liquid.
- Increase the amount of salt.
- During periods of warm weather with high humidity, use less water and cooler water.

Bread does not rise:
- Did you forget yeast?
- Decrease the amount of flour.
- Have liquids at 80° F, all other ingredients at room temperature.
- Increase the amount of sugar.
- Check activity of yeast.

Loaf is short and dense:
- Check consistency of dough after 5 minutes into the kneading time. If dough is too dry, add liquid, 1 tablespoon at a time.
- Use high protein bread flour.
- Certain flours, such as whole wheat and rye, create heavier products than white flour.

Bread has a coarse texture:
- Decrease the amount of liquid.
- Increase the amount of salt.

Bread has a doughy center:
- Decrease the amount of liquid.
- Check yeast activity.
- Bread machine may be malfunctioning; check user's manual.

Unbrowned top:
- Increase the amount of sugar.
- Select a smaller size recipe.
- If the machine has an all-glass top, tent outside of dome with foil.

Large mushroom top:
- Decrease the amount of water.
- Decrease the amount of yeast.

Index